# THE BOOK OF
# JOB

# THE
# BOOK OF JOB

Edited with an Introduction

by

A. NAIRNE, D.D.

CAMBRIDGE
AT THE UNIVERSITY PRESS
1935

CAMBRIDGE UNIVERSITY PRESS
Cambridge, New York, Melbourne, Madrid, Cape Town,
Singapore, São Paulo, Delhi, Mexico City

Cambridge University Press
The Edinburgh Building, Cambridge CB2 8RU, UK

Published in the United States of America by Cambridge University Press, New York

www.cambridge.org
Information on this title: www.cambridge.org/9781107682443

First published 1935
First paperback edition 2013

*A catalogue record for this publication is available from the British Library*

ISBN 978-1-107-68244-3 Paperback

# ILLUSTRATIONS

from the engravings by William Blake

# INTRODUCTION

A BIBLE is an edited collection of sacred writings ancient and modern. The Hebrew Bible is in three volumes, Law Prophets Writings. The Law contains what are called The five Books of Moses in the English version. The Prophets contain the prophetical histories, Joshua Judges Samuel Kings, and the Books of Isaiah Jeremiah Ezekiel with The XII (or Minor Prophets). Chronicles Ezra Nehemiah and Daniel, belong to the Writings, with the rest of the books which in the English Bible are translated from the Hebrew. Our Apocrypha represents the additions which were read in their Septuagint, or Greek Bible, by the Jewish Church at Alexandria. For the rest of the Old Testament our A.V. and R.V. are translated directly from the Hebrew, but follow the arrangement of the Septuagint which had been conserved in the Latin Vulgate, the heritage of the medieval Church in the West. This obscures the indications of date which the three volumes of the Hebrew Bible afford, and also creates prejudices about authorship concerning which the Septuagint makes many assertions where the Hebrew is silent. The Hebrew has no such title as The five Books of Moses, nor does it tell anything about the date or provenance of Job. To speak generally, the Hebrew Bible leaves large freedom for exercise of Higher Criticism.

Indeed its three volumes indicate roughly the same dates for whole classes of books as criticism discovers. The Law is a collection made by the Jewish Church and ratified as canonical during the Captivity, as the narrative of Ezra tells. The Prophets were afterwards combined with the Law, though old-fashioned Jews (Sadducees) did not recognise their canonical value. This Prophetical collection, including with the Prophecies the Prophetical Histories, invests those Histories with historical authority superior to the ecclesiastical retrospect of Chronicles. As to the Scriptures, S. Luke xxiv suggests that in the first century A.D. these were still outside the Apostolic Bible, except the Psalms, the Prayer Book of the Synagogue, to which with Law and Prophets the risen Lord appeals when he explains the sufferings of Messiah to the disciples on the road to Emmaus.

The Exile was the Bible-making era. Bible-making was collecting selecting editing. The Law was the final edition of age-old continuously developed law and historical tradition. The Prophets were the collected arranged and edited historical documents of the monarchic period, and the most precious part of that collection were the Prophets' own utterances, together with echoes from their successors and notes of narrative and liturgic hymns: fragrant readings for synagogue devotion. The Writings included Psalms Proverbs, collections of ancient poetry and wisdom combined with later work of like kind and tinged with contemporary feeling.

On the whole this volume of the Jewish Bible represents the mind of the Exile; the most likely date for the composition of any book in this volume is the Exile; and Job may be thus dated.

This period was largely dominated by the Law; but far from wholly so. Faith in one true living God, for which Prophets had contended as it seemed in vain, was now the religion of Israel. The Prophets might seem in their own days to fail: but Israel was deaf to their doctrine because Israel was playing so strenuously a warrior nation's part in making history. That history, in its deed and suffering, clashed and combined with the prophetic preaching to create a new heart in the period of defeat reflection penitence and hope. Through the exilic and post-exilic era Israel was broadening and burgeoning. The Jewish Church was inaugurated and devoted to the proper work of the Church, worship scholarship salvation of the heathen, trust in God's purpose for the world and in the vocation of God's chosen people to carry out his purpose; and all this practically ordered and organised by Law, divine law, The Law of the LORD by the hand of Moses.

Law as a bond of unity and permanence holds together the variety of exilic faith. The Psalter is the symbol of a deeper union, the catholic piety of all pure souls. Another element is Apocalypse, that impulse of a later Prophecy toward a more definite Messianic hope and therewith to that concentration of eternal life into such a doctrine of resurrection as appears in Daniel.

Yet another is the rewriting of ancient history and its completion by contemporary record, as in Chronicles Ezra Nehemiah. And yet another is the reflective questioning Wisdom literature to which the book of Job belongs. This Wisdom, the philosophy of the Hebrews, was no new thing. In certain Psalms and Proverbs earlier forms of its expression are preserved, but it deepened and widened in the exilic period. It cared but secondarily for law and ritual. It recognised the piety of other nations, the naturally Christian souls. It delighted in the life and mystery of bird and beast and plant, in the loveliness and terrors of creation. It tolerated criticism of orthodox beliefs: in the words of an old-fashioned Jew, who was not a friend to all the new ideas, it put truth above all else and would strive for it unto death. And yet, as the Psalter drew all hearts together by the Spirit of worship, so charity directed truth in all disputes of Schools. The men of Wisdom were gentle scholars who listened to the still sad music of humanity, yet stood forth uncompromising champions of the oppressed and defenders of perplexed conscience and sometimes of moral failures. They were S. Lukes of the Old Testament. Into this class, exilic Wisdom interacting with various literary habits of the long exilic period, the Book of Job seems to fall quite naturally.

Job is an old story which has been refashioned to new purpose. It had always reached beyond the Hebrew nation: Job is of Uz, his Friends from the wide wise

East. In the poem of the Captivity Job himself may sometimes remind us of afflicted Israel and the suffering Servant of the LORD, but he is rather a symbol of Mansoul, of his doubtful doom and his dependence on God.

The poem enlarges deepens purifies the idea of God. Even Prophets had proclaimed Jahveh, the LORD, too naively, like an earthly king, though King of kings: only in some chapters of the latter part of Isaiah is there anything quite like that divine infinity, out of which flows Job's conversion: the poem is the story of the new creation of what is described in the 1st Epistle of S. Peter as "conscience of God".

The story is a story. Job stands as symbol yet is vividly presented as a person. Actual events conversations characters form the theme through which strange harmonies develop. As in *Paradise Lost* the meaning is a battle for the soul of man, but that meaning emerges from the adventures of protagonists in heaven and earth which engross our wondering expectation.

This is the plan of the Book:

(I) Prologue. A scholar's adaptation of Hebrew folklore to a poetic dream shews Jahveh as King holding court in heaven. Sons of God, the guild of ministering angels, attend. The Satan—a title not a proper name—the Adversary, no malignant rebel but the Trier of Mansoul, comes with the rest, and is commissioned to try Job, a saint worth trial to the uttermost. Then Job's afflictions crowd upon him. His three Friends come to comfort him, Eliphaz the gentle, Bildad the learned, Zophar rough and glib of tongue.

(II) The fourfold argument in three rounds of interlocution between Job and the three Friends. The language rises from the plain narrative of Prologue to rhythmic grandeur, which Job enriches with ever deeper thought and bolder sincerity as he interposes between the successive orations of the Friends, turning more and more away from them to God, estranged though God seems to persist. In the first round the Friends offer the conventional assurance of popular theology that no good man can succumb to evil at the good hand of God. But Job's downright refusal to allow this trust which experience contradicts brings (2) the reflection that no man is truly good; that Job shares the common guilt of original sin; his claim to be blameless is itself sinful; hence his affliction. Again Job's fierce protest, with his mysterious appeal to God against God, God within against God in appearance, leads to (3) accusation of Job as guilty of definite and serious wickedness. Job rebuts the charge, not without wrath against the Friends and God. Bildad concludes in a short speech of dignity beauty and reverence. Zophar is already silenced and Job usurps his turn, repeating the denunciations Zophar had poured forth and applying these to the Friends themselves as the real sinners who will find a nemesis indeed.

Then (III) Job "takes up his own parable", opening with a lyric Hymn of Wisdom, in which he sings the mystery of God's transcendence in calmer strain part hopeful part resigned wholly yearning. Thence he passes into solemn declaration of innocence, and appeals to God for answer.

And (IV) the LORD answers out of the tempest, bidding Job set his littleness over against the immensity of the universe, yet testifying to a divine lovingkindness which cares for beasts as well as men. And Job submits. But the LORD goes on and pictures—for his admiration or humiliation, at any rate for his conscience sake the two huge brutes Leviathan and Behemoth—and now Job is humbled to the dust yet cleaves not to it. He survives weak but new born: the drama of a soul's conversion is finished.

Only a happy Epilogue is added (V): Job's restoration to the visible favour of God; like the Prologue a piece of the old story, and written like the Prologue in a scholar's delightful simplified prose.

This adaptation in Prologue and Epilogue of old tradition, its artistic juncture with the dialectic, "that conversation between friends directed to a noble end", is part of a reflective subtlety which characterises dates and influences the poem.

An example will explain. Job's oracle in chapter xix has been interpreted as certain hope of life beyond the grave wherein, without flesh but in undying spirit, he will enjoy vindication; or as a still bolder hope that from the resurrection of his very flesh he shall enjoy it; or simply

that he will recover from his illness and plainly see
retribution fall upon his Friends. The word Goel, redeemer or avenger, is also ambiguous. It was a fierce
term in ancient days for the Blood-avenger of tribal
feud. In one of the three interpretations of the whole
passage it would bear just that meaning, whether
applied to God or perhaps not even so transformed. In
the other two it is certainly applied to God and takes a
far more august significance.

But repeated meditation on the whole passage makes
such question secondary. The deep thing is that the
old word, sudden and fierce in first utterance, becomes
mysteriously holy in the reverie to which the outburst
grows. And so with the rest. Fears hopes questionings,
from Sheol and the Pit to Resurrection preached by
Pharisees, disturbed the mind of the Exile. But Job's
passion transcends such religiosities. He yearns for
union with God. That union is the final end of the
story; Paradise Lost and Regained.

The linguistic style is in keeping; vigorous terse
luminous, worthy of the best age of Hebrew, it has been
credited to an early date. Whether any modern hebraist
can infer so nicely is doubtful, but there seems a dif-
ference between the exilic scholar's literary skill and
the free lyric of Isaiah of Jerusalem or the author of
Psalm civ.

This does not apply to chapters xxxii–xxxvii in which
Elihu discourses. These are strangely writ, hard to
translate, in some places hard to recognise as Hebrew

at all. Some fine phrases in A.V. and R.V. are hazar-
dously derived from a possibly corrupt but more likely
a clumsy original. Elihu interrupts the drama. Jahveh
notices him not, Job and his Friends ignore him. He is
introduced as a younger man, and that may be a hint
that the episode has been added to the book. How,
when, by whom, it is vain to guess. He throws little
light on the indomitable faith of Job or the perversity of
the Friends. He would supersede their old-fashioned
doctrine of retribution by one of remedial chastisement.
That gives him occasion to say some beautiful things in
the Spirit of the Exhortation in the Visitation of the Sick
in the Book of Common Prayer, but he is far from the
firm lines of that happy gospelling.

Some may think that chapters xl, xli are also super-
fluous, a rhetorical exercise spoiling Jahveh's answer.
But this rhetoric is no mere exercise. The Hebrew is
magnificent. The passage from simple nature to nature
touched with mythology is in keeping with the student-
taste which characterises the poet and partly indicates
his date. And there is more than student-taste: there is
theology and inspiration. The tremendous element in
the divine care and purpose of Creation, and the im-
potence of men in the midst of such sacramental
mystery, was needed to evoke Job's complete conversion, and however alien to a modern treatise of divinity,
it also served to complete the poet's doctrine of God.

Two terms are used. In Prologue Epilogue and in the

divine answer from the tempest Jahveh is a proper name, the Name of the God of Israel, in later times though written never pronounced in reading Scripture, Adonai being read instead. Adonai was translated Kyrios and Dominus in the Greek and Latin Bibles, and that is represented in the English Bible by The LORD in capital letters, though in a few places Jehovah imperfectly indicates the Hebrew word. The other term, Elohim, is translated God. This is not a proper name but a noun in the plural which perhaps points back to earlier reverence towards the Spirits of fire flood and air, the Angels of Psalm civ, forces of Nature as we more prosaically speak. The Sons of God in the Prologue are this holy array collectively. But Elohim, in its supreme significance as God, means, more than the sum, the essentially divine source and sway of all, the One God of universal nature, of world-wide worship, the Creator. Such God did Israel's nomad ancestors worship, however imperfectly, in the desert. His temple was the all-supernal sky. No form no name was his: "I am that I am", he (not Jahveh) answered Moses. Such God no man hath seen, but in the tempest he manifested his presence. The thunder cloud was his pavilion. He rode on the angels of wind. Seraphs of fire went forth from him, and his voice was thunder. This explains the overpowering glory of Nature in the divine answer to Job from the storm. The poet carries back to the unsophisticated space of ancient religion, clearing away the imitation of human passions with which the Friends attenuate it. Not Jahveh, King of Israel, favourer of the elect, bound to morality by rule, not such is God above all gods, Very God. And yet at last the poet does bring in Jahveh. But it is as when the Lord Jesus bids us pray to "Our Father, which art in heaven"—a cordial metaphysic. For the Name reveals the person, vivifies the idea, and as in Isaiah xl ff. is purified of limitations. The Creator is the sustainer who cares for his creatures, cares for Job. Yet his care is no petty sentiment. Man and beast, Job and Leviathan, the Very God himself, are devoted to the All beyond the selves. And Job wakes to a new mind, in dust and ashes but in communion with the One True Living God; even as a bubble on the stream of his infinite purpose, yet at one with the stream. And so the Epic closes in lovingkindness: the child has come home to the Father of all.

That is the Epic of Job; no analysis of the problem of pain, nor justification of the way of God toward man, but the story of the conversion of a soul, to be read with anxious expectation of the issue and that sympathy which man's natural yearning for God provokes.

To that end this Introduction has been somewhat discursively composed. Few notes will be given with the text. Renan's version, in scholarly French, without adornment or annotation, holds readers by its uninterrupted flow, and offers a pattern of arrangement in a few large masses. In this homely edition alternative renderings, geographical historical critical explanations will be eschewed. The text will be taken from the English R.V., but its marginal renderings will be adopted without comment where necessary*. That this is often necessary is shewn by Dr Driver in his very perfect small edition, than which no better guide can be desired by plain readers who wish to clear away linguistic or theological difficulties. Minute students will turn to Driver's larger edition (in Clark's International Critical Series) or the elaborate and masterful commentary of C. J. Ball (Clarendon Press).

For readers of this pocket companion to the poem as a poem, the story as a story, sacred and inspiring, no further aids need be mentioned except that series of engravings which William Blake has left as the very crown of his poetic art. The series is given in reduced scale in Gilchrist's *Life of Blake*, with valuable comment by Rossetti.

A. N.

WINDSOR
*September* 1935

* A list of these adoptions may be useful:

| | | | |
|---|---|---|---|
| xii. 6 | xx. 20 | xxvi. 5 | xxxvi. 16 |
| xiii. 14–19 | xxi. 24 | xxx. 24 | ,,    18 |
| xv. 20 | ,,  30 | xxxi. 33 | xxxvii. 23 |
| xviii. 14 | xxiii. 10 | xxxiv. 14 | xxxviii. 36 |
| xix. 7 | ,,    12 | ,,   18 f. | xxxix. 24 |
| ,,  17 | ,,    17 | ,,    24 | xlii. 6 |
| ,,  28 | xxiv. 18 | | |

Then went Satan forth from the presence of the Lord

# THE
# BOOK OF JOB

There was a man in the land of Uz, whose name In the Presence of Jahveh Job is committed to the Adversary for trial of his integrity
was Job; and that man was perfect and upright, and
one that feared God, and eschewed evil. And there
were born unto him seven sons and three daughters.
His substance also was seven thousand sheep, and
three thousand camels, and five hundred yoke of
oxen, and five hundred she-asses, and a very great
household; so that this man was the greatest of all the
children of the east. And his sons went and held a
feast in the house of each one upon his day; and they
sent and called for their three sisters to eat and to
drink with them. And it was so, when the days of
their feasting were gone about, that Job sent and
sanctified them, and rose up early in the morning,
and offered burnt offerings according to the number
of them all: for Job said, It may be that my sons have
sinned, and renounced God in their hearts. Thus did
Job continually.

Now there was a day when the sons of God came
to present themselves before the LORD, and Satan
came also among them. And the LORD said unto
Satan, Whence comest thou? Then Satan answered
the LORD, and said, From going to and fro in the
earth, and from walking up and down in it. And the
LORD said unto Satan, Hast thou considered my servant Job? for there is none like him in the earth, a

perfect and an upright man, one that feareth God, and escheweth evil. Then Satan answered the LORD, and said, Doth Job fear God for nought? Hast not thou made an hedge about him, and about his house, and about all that he hath, on every side? thou hast blessed the work of his hands, and his substance is increased in the land. But put forth thine hand now, and touch all that he hath, and he will renounce thee to thy face. And the LORD said unto Satan, Behold, all that he hath is in thy power; only upon himself put not forth thine hand. So Satan went forth from the presence of the LORD.

And it fell on a day when his sons and his daughters were eating and drinking wine in their eldest brother's house, that there came a messenger unto Job, and said, The oxen were plowing, and the asses feeding beside them: and the Sabeans fell upon them, and took them away; yea, they have slain the servants with the edge of the sword; and I only am escaped alone to tell thee. While he was yet speaking, there came also another, and said, The fire of God is fallen from heaven, and hath burned up the sheep, and the servants, and consumed them; and I only am escaped alone to tell thee. While he was yet speaking, there came also another, and said, The Chaldeans made three bands, and fell upon the camels, and have taken them away, yea, and slain the servants with the edge of the sword; and I only am escaped alone to tell thee. While he was yet speaking, there came also another, and said, Thy sons and thy daughters were eating and drinking wine in their eldest brother's house: and, behold, there came a great wind from the wilderness, and smote the four corners of the house, and it fell upon the young men, and they are dead; and I only am escaped alone to tell thee. Then Job arose, and rent his mantle, and shaved his head, and fell down upon the ground, and worshipped; and he said, Naked came I out of my mother's womb, and naked shall I return thither: the LORD gave, and the LORD hath taken away; blessed be the name of the LORD. In all this Job sinned not, nor charged God with foolishness.

Again there was a day when the sons of God came to present themselves before the LORD, and Satan came also among them to present himself before the LORD. And the LORD said unto Satan, From whence comest thou? And Satan answered the LORD, and said, From going to and fro in the earth, and from walking up and down in it. And the LORD said unto Satan, Hast thou considered my servant Job? for there is none like him in the earth, a perfect and an upright man, one that feareth God, and escheweth evil: and he still holdeth fast his integrity, although thou movedst me against him, to destroy him without cause. And Satan answered the LORD, and said, Skin for skin, yea, all that a man hath will he give for his life. But put forth thine hand now, and touch his bone and his flesh, and he will renounce thee to thy face. And the LORD said unto Satan, Behold, he is in thine hand; only spare his life. So Satan went forth from the presence of the LORD, and smote Job with sore boils from the sole of his foot unto his crown. And he took him a potsherd to scrape himself withal;

and he sat among the ashes. Then said his wife unto him, Dost thou still hold fast thine integrity? renounce God, and die. But he said unto her, Thou speakest as one of the foolish women speaketh. What? shall we receive good at the hand of God, and shall we not receive evil? In all this did not Job sin with his lips.

Three Friends come to comfort Job in his affliction

Now when Job's three friends heard of all this evil that was come upon him, they came every one from his own place; Eliphaz the Temanite, and Bildad the Shuhite, and Zophar the Naamathite: and they made an appointment together to come to bemoan him and to comfort him. And when they lifted up their eyes afar off, and knew him not, they lifted up their voice, and wept; and they rent every one his mantle, and sprinkled dust upon their heads toward heaven. So they sat down with him upon the ground seven days and seven nights, and none spake a word unto him: for they saw that his grief was very great.

Job, ignorant of the divine transaction, curses his birth day

After this opened Job his mouth, and cursed his day. And Job answered and said:

Let the day perish wherein I was born,
And the night which said, There is a man child
    conceived.
Let that day be darkness;
Let not God regard it from above,
Neither let the light shine upon it.
Let darkness and the shadow of death claim it for
    their own;
Let a cloud dwell upon it;
Let all that maketh black the day terrify it.

As for that night, let thick darkness seize upon it:
Let it not rejoice among the days of the year;
Let it not come into the number of the months.
Lo, let that night be barren;
Let no joyful voice come therein.
Let them curse it that curse the day,
Who are ready to rouse up leviathan.
Let the stars of the twilight thereof be dark:
Let it look for light, but have none;
Neither let it behold the eyelids of the morning:
Because it shut not up the doors of my mother's
    womb,
Nor hid trouble from mine eyes.
Why died I not from the womb?
Why did I not give up the ghost when I came out of
    the belly?
Why did the knees receive me?
Or why the breasts, that I should suck?
For now should I have lien down and been quiet;
I should have slept; then had I been at rest:
With kings and counsellors of the earth,
Which built up waste places for themselves;
Or with princes that had gold,
Who filled their houses with silver:
Or as an hidden untimely birth I had not been;
As infants which never saw light.
There the wicked cease from troubling;
And there the weary be at rest.
There the prisoners are at ease together;
They hear not the voice of the taskmaster.
The small and great are there;

And the servant is free from his master.
Wherefore is light given to him that is in misery,
And life unto the bitter in soul;
Which long for death, but it cometh not;
And dig for it more than for hid treasures;
Which rejoice exceedingly,
And are glad, when they can find the grave?
Why is light given to a man whose way is hid,
And whom God hath hedged in?
For my sighing cometh before I eat,
And my roarings are poured out like water.
For the thing which I fear cometh upon me,
And that which I am afraid of cometh unto me.
I am not at ease, neither am I quiet, neither have I
    rest;
But trouble cometh.

Eliphaz bids
Job have
confidence in
God, as a good
man may;

Then answered Eliphaz the Temanite, and said,
If one assay to commune with thee, wilt thou be
    grieved?
But who can withhold himself from speaking?
Behold, thou hast instructed many,
And thou hast strengthened the weak hands.
Thy words have upholden him that was falling,
And thou hast confirmed the feeble knees.
But now it is come unto thee, and thou faintest;
It toucheth thee, and thou art troubled.
Is not thy fear of God thy confidence,
And thy hope the integrity of thy ways?
Remember, I pray thee, who ever perished, being
    innocent?

Or where were the upright cut off?
According as I have seen, they that plow iniquity,
And sow trouble, reap the same.
By the breath of God they perish,
And by the blast of his anger are they consumed.
The roaring of the lion, and the voice of the fierce lion,
And the teeth of the young lions, are broken.
The old lion perisheth for lack of prey,
And the whelps of the lioness are scattered abroad.
Now a thing was secretly brought to me,
And mine ear received a whisper thereof.
In thoughts from the visions of the night,
When deep sleep falleth on men,
Fear came upon me, and trembling,
Which made all my bones to shake.
Then a spirit passed before my face;
The hair of my flesh stood up.
It stood still, but I could not discern the appearance *yet remembering the frailty of human virtue,*
    thereof;
A form was before mine eyes:
There was silence, and I heard a voice, saying,
Shall mortal man be more just than God?
Shall a man be more pure than his Maker?
Behold, he putteth no trust in his servants;
And his angels he chargeth with folly:
How much more them that dwell in houses of clay,
Whose foundation is in the dust,
Which are crushed before the moth!
Betwixt morning and evening they are destroyed:
They perish for ever without any regarding it.
Is not their tent-cord plucked up within them?

They die, and that without wisdom.
Call now; is there any that will answer thee?
And to which of the holy ones wilt thou turn?
For vexation killeth the foolish man,
And jealousy slayeth the silly one.
I have seen the foolish taking root:
But suddenly I cursed his habitation.
His children are far from safety,
And they are crushed in the gate,
Neither is there any to deliver them.
Whose harvest the hungry eateth up,
And taketh it even out of the thorns,
And the snare gapeth for their substance.
For affliction cometh not forth of the dust,
Neither doth trouble spring out of the ground;
But man is born unto trouble,
As the sparks fly upward.

would have him seek unto God more suppliantly
But as for me, I would seek unto God,
And unto God would I commit my cause:
Which doeth great things and unsearchable;
Marvellous things without number:
Who giveth rain upon the earth,
And sendeth waters upon the fields:
So that he setteth up on high those that be low;
And those which mourn are exalted to safety.
He frustrateth the devices of the crafty,
So that their hands cannot perform their enterprise.
He taketh the wise in their own craftiness:
And the counsel of the froward is carried headlong.
They meet with darkness in the day-time,
And grope at noonday as in the night.

But he saveth from the sword of their mouth,
Even the needy from the hand of the mighty.
So the poor hath hope,
And iniquity stoppeth her mouth.
Behold, happy is the man whom God correcteth:
Therefore despise not thou the chastening of the
   Almighty.
For he maketh sore, and bindeth up;
He woundeth, and his hands make whole.
He shall deliver thee in six troubles;
Yea, in seven there shall no evil touch thee.
In famine he shall redeem thee from death;
And in war from the power of the sword.
Thou shalt be hid from the scourge of the tongue;
Neither shalt thou be afraid of destruction when it
   cometh.
At destruction and dearth thou shalt laugh;
Neither shalt thou be afraid of the beasts of the earth.
For thou shalt be in league with the stones of the field;
And the beasts of the field shall be at peace with thee.
And thou shalt know that thy tent is in peace;
And thou shalt visit thy fold, and shalt miss nothing.
Thou shalt know also that thy seed shall be great,
And thine offspring as the grass of the earth.
Thou shalt come to thy grave in a full age,
Like as a shock of corn cometh in in its season.
Lo this, we have searched it, so it is;
Hear it, and know thou it for thy good.

Then Job answered and said,
Oh that my vexation were but weighed,

From such
cold comfort
and unfriendly
friendship

And my calamity laid in the balances together!
For now it would be heavier than the sand of the seas:
Therefore have my words been rash.
For the arrows of the Almighty are within me,
The poison whereof my spirit drinketh up:
The terrors of God do set themselves in array against
    me.
Doth the wild ass bray when he hath grass?
Or loweth the ox over his fodder?
Can that which hath no savour be eaten without salt?
Or is there any taste in the white of an egg?
My soul refuseth to touch them;
They are as loathsome meat to me.
Oh that I might have my request;

Job doth turn
to God,

And that God would grant me the thing that I long
    for!
Even that it would please God to crush me;
That he would let loose his hand, and cut me off!
Then should I yet have comfort;
Yea, I would exult in pain that spareth not:
For I have not denied the words of the Holy One.
What is my strength, that I should wait?
And what is mine end, that I should be patient?
Is my strength the strength of stones?
Or is my flesh of brass?
Is it not that I have no help in me,
And that effectual working is driven quite from me?
To him that is ready to faint kindness should be
    shewed from his friend;
Even to him that forsaketh the fear of the Almighty.
My brethren have dealt deceitfully as a brook,

As the channel of brooks that pass away;
Which are black by reason of the ice,
And wherein the snow hideth itself:
What time they wax warm, they vanish:
When it is hot, they are consumed out of their place.
The caravans that travel by the way of them turn
     aside;
They go up into the waste, and perish.
The caravans of Tema looked,
The companies of Sheba waited for them.
They were ashamed because they had hoped;
They came thither, and were confounded.
For now ye are nothing;
Ye see a terror, and are afraid.
Did I say, Give unto me?
Or, Offer a present for me of your substance?
Or, Deliver me from the adversary's hand?
Or, Redeem me from the hand of the oppressors?
Teach me, and I will hold my peace:
And cause me to understand wherein I have erred.
How forcible are words of uprightness!
But what doth your arguing reprove?
Do ye imagine to reprove words?
Seeing that the speeches of one that is desperate are
     as wind.
Yea, ye would cast lots upon the fatherless,
And make merchandise of your friend.
Now therefore be pleased to look upon me;
For surely I shall not lie to your face.
Return, I pray you, let there be no injustice;
Yea, return again, my cause is righteous.

Is there injustice on my tongue?
Cannot my taste discern mischievous things?
but in bitter
perplexity Is there not a warfare to man upon earth?
And are not his days like the days of an hireling?
As a servant that earnestly desireth the shadow,
And as an hireling that looketh for his wages:
So am I made to possess months of vanity,
And wearisome nights are appointed to me.
When I lie down, I say,
When shall I arise? but the night is long;
And I am full of tossings to and fro unto the dawning
    of the day.
My flesh is clothed with worms and clods of dust;
My skin closeth up and breaketh out afresh.
My days are swifter than a weaver's shuttle,
And are spent without hope.
Oh remember that my life is wind:
Mine eye shall no more see good.
The eye of him that seeth me shall behold me no more:
Thine eyes shall be upon me, but I shall not be.
As the cloud is consumed and vanisheth away,
So he that goeth down to Sheol* shall come up no
    more.
He shall return no more to his house,
Neither shall his place know him any more.
Therefore I will not refrain my mouth;
I will speak in the anguish of my spirit;
I will complain in the bitterness of my soul.
Am I a sea, or a sea-monster,
That thou settest a watch over me?

    * Or The Grave: from the language of Hebrew myth.

When I say, My bed shall comfort me,
My couch shall ease my complaint;
Then thou scarest me with dreams,
And terrifiest me through visions:
So that my soul chooseth strangling,
And death rather than these my bones.
I loathe my life; I would not live alway:
Let me alone; for my days are vanity.
What is man, that thou shouldest magnify him,
And that thou shouldest set thine heart upon him,
And that thou shouldest visit him every morning,
And try him every moment?
How long wilt thou not look away from me,
Nor let me alone till I swallow down my spittle?
If I have sinned, what do I unto thee, O thou watcher
    of men?
Why hast thou set me as a mark for thee,
So that I am a burden to myself?
And why dost thou not pardon my transgression, and
    take away mine iniquity?
For now shall I lie down in the dust;
And thou shalt seek me diligently, but I shall not
    be.

Then answered Bildad the Shuhite, and said,
How long wilt thou speak these things?
And how long shall the words of thy mouth be like a
    mighty wind?
Doth God pervert judgement?
Or doth the Almighty pervert justice?
If thy children have sinned against him,

Bildad bids Job
trust the
wisdom of the
ancients: God
is always just,
visiting sin on
sinners—For
thee, friend
Job, good man,
joy returneth

And he have delivered them into the hand of their
    transgression:
If thou wouldest seek diligently unto God,
And make thy supplication to the Almighty;
If thou wert pure and upright;
Surely now he would awake for thee,
And make the habitation of thy righteousness pro-
    sperous.
And though thy beginning was small,
Yet thy latter end should greatly increase.
For inquire, I pray thee, of the former age,
And apply thyself to that which their fathers have
    searched out:
(For we are but of yesterday, and know nothing,
Because our days upon earth are a shadow:)
Shall not they teach thee, and tell thee,
And utter words out of their heart?
Can the rush grow up without mire?
Can the flag grow without water?
Whilst it is yet in its greenness, and not cut down,
It withereth before any other herb.
So are the paths of all that forget God;
And the hope of the godless man shall perish:
Whose confidence shall break in sunder,
And whose trust is a spider's web.
He shall lean upon his house, but it shall not stand:
He shall hold fast thereby, but it shall not endure.
He is green before the sun,
And his shoots go forth over his garden.
His roots are wrapped about the heap,
He beholdeth the place of stones.

If he be destroyed from his place,
Then it shall deny him, saying, I have not seen thee.
Behold, this is the joy of his way,
And out of the earth shall others spring.
Behold, God will not cast away a perfect man,
Neither will he uphold the evil-doers.
He will yet fill thy mouth with laughter,
And thy lips with shouting.
They that hate thee shall be clothed with shame;
And the tent of the wicked shall be no more.

Then Job answered and said,
Of a truth I know that it is so:
But how can man be just with God?
If he be pleased to contend with him,
He cannot answer him one of a thousand.
He is wise in heart, and mighty in strength:
Who hath hardened himself against him, and pro-
    spered?
Which removeth the mountains, and they know it not,
When he overturneth them in his anger.
Which shaketh the earth out of her place,
And the pillars thereof tremble.
Which commandeth the sun, and it riseth not;
And sealeth up the stars.
Which alone stretcheth out the heavens,
And treadeth upon the waves of the sea.
Which maketh the Bear, Orion, and the Pleiades,
And the chambers of the south.
Which doeth great things past finding out;
Yea, marvellous things without number.

Job answers,
Yes: yet God
is against me:
perfect or
guilty God
destroys both:
if not He, who
doth it?

Lo, he goeth by me, and I see him not:
He passeth on also, but I perceive him not.
Behold, he seizeth the prey, who can hinder him?
Who will say unto him, What doest thou?
God will not withdraw his anger;
The helpers of Rahab* do stoop under him.
How much less shall I answer him,
And choose out my words to reason with him?
Whom, though I were righteous, yet would I not
    answer;
I would make supplication to mine adversary.
If I had called, and he had answered me;
Yet would I not believe that he hearkened unto my
    voice.
For he breaketh me with a tempest,
And multiplieth my wounds without cause.
He will not suffer me to take my breath,
But filleth me with bitterness.
If we speak of the strength of the mighty, lo, he is
    there!
And if of judgement, who will appoint me a time?
Though I be righteous, mine own mouth shall con-
    demn me:
Though I be perfect, it shall prove me perverse.
I am perfect; I regard not myself;
I despise my life.
It is all one; therefore I say,
He destroyeth the perfect and the wicked.
If the scourge slay suddenly,

* Or Arrogancy: see Is. xxx. 7, li. 9: a term from
Hebrew mythology.

He will mock at the trial of the innocent.
The earth is given into the hand of the wicked:
He covereth the faces of the judges thereof;
If it be not he, who then is it?
Now my days are swifter than a post:
They flee away, they see no good.
They are passed away as the swift ships:
As the eagle that swoopeth on the prey.
If I say, I will forget my complaint,
I will put off my sad countenance, and be of good
    cheer:
I am afraid of all my sorrows,
I know that thou wilt not hold me innocent.
I shall be condemned;
Why then do I labour in vain?
If I wash myself with snow water,
And make my hands never so clean;
Yet wilt thou plunge me in the ditch,
And mine own clothes shall abhor me.
For he is not a man, as I am, that I should answer
    him,
That we should come together in judgement.
There is no daysman betwixt us,
That might lay his hand upon us both.
Let him take his rod away from me,
And let not his terror make me afraid:
Then would I speak, and not fear him;
For I am not so in myself.
My soul is weary of my life;
I will give free course to my complaint;
I will speak in the bitterness of my soul.

I will say unto God, Do not condemn me;
Shew me wherefore thou contendest with me.
Is it good unto thee that thou shouldest oppress,
That thou shouldest despise the work of thine hands,
And shine upon the counsel of the wicked?
Hast thou eyes of flesh,
Or seest thou as man seeth?
Are thy days as the days of man,
Or thy years as man's days,
That thou inquirest after mine iniquity,
And searchest after my sin,
Although thou knowest that I am not wicked;
And there is none that can deliver out of thine hand?

*God's awful providence, creating and preserving for the day of calamity*

Thine hands have framed me and fashioned me
Together round about; yet thou dost destroy me.
Remember, I beseech thee, that thou hast fashioned
    me as clay;
And wilt thou bring me into dust again?
Hast thou not poured me out as milk,
And curdled me like cheese?
Thou hast clothed me with skin and flesh,
And knit me together with bones and sinews.
Thou hast granted me life and favour,
And thy visitation hath preserved my spirit.
Yet these things thou didst hide in thine heart;
I know that this is with thee:
If I sin, then thou markest me,
And thou wilt not acquit me from mine iniquity.
If I be wicked, woe unto me;
And if I be righteous, yet shall I not lift up my head;
Being filled with ignominy

And looking upon mine affliction.
And if my head exalt itself, thou huntest me as a
    lion:
And again thou shewest thyself marvellous upon me.
Thou renewest thy witnesses against me,
And increasest thine indignation upon me;
Changes and warfare are with me.
Wherefore then hast thou brought me forth out of
    the womb?
I had given up the ghost, and no eye had seen me.
I should have been as though I had not been;
I should have been carried from the womb to the
    grave.
Are not my days few? cease then,
And let me alone, that I may take comfort a little,
Before I go whence I shall not return,
Even to the land of darkness and of the shadow of
    death;
A land of thick darkness, as darkness itself;
A land of the shadow of death, without any order,
And where the light is as darkness.


Then answered Zophar the Naamathite, and said, *Ah! the wicked*
Should not the multitude of words be answered? *words! cries*
And should a man full of talk be justified? *Zophar: O Job,*
*repentance is*
Should thy boastings make men hold their peace? *thy need*
And when thou mockest, shall no man make thee
    ashamed?
For thou sayest, My doctrine is pure,
And I am clean in thine eyes.
But Oh that God would speak,

And open his lips against thee;
And that he would shew thee the secrets of wisdom,
That it is manifold in effectual working!
Know therefore that God exacteth of thee less than
    thine iniquity deserveth.
Canst thou by searching find out God?
Canst thou find out the Almighty unto perfection?
It is high as heaven; what canst thou do?
Deeper than Sheol; what canst thou know?
The measure thereof is longer than the earth,
And broader than the sea.
If he pass through, and shut up,
And call unto judgement, then who can hinder him?
For he knoweth vain men:
He seeth iniquity also, even though he consider it
    not.
But vain man is void of understanding,
Yea, man is born as a wild ass's colt.
If thou set thine heart aright,
And stretch out thine hands toward him;
If iniquity be in thine hand, put it far away,
And let not unrighteousness dwell in thy tents;
Surely then shalt thou lift up thy face without
    spot;
Yea, thou shalt be stedfast, and shalt not fear:
For thou shalt forget thy misery;
Thou shalt remember it as waters that are passed
    away:
And thy life shall be clearer than the noonday;
Though there be darkness, it shall be as the morning.
And thou shalt be secure, because there is hope;

Yea, thou shalt search about thee, and shalt take thy
    rest in safety.
Also thou shalt lie down, and none shall make thee
    afraid;
Yea, many shall make suit unto thee.
But the eyes of the wicked shall fail,
And they shall have no way to flee,
And their hope shall be the giving up of the ghost.

Then Job answered and said,
No doubt but ye are the people,
And wisdom shall die with you.
But I have understanding as well as you;
I am not inferior to you:
Yea, who knoweth not such things as these?
I am as one that is a laughing-stock to his neighbour,
A man that called upon God, and he answered him:
The just, the perfect man is a laughing-stock.
In the thought of him that is at ease there is contempt
    for misfortune;
It is ready for them whose foot slippeth.
The tents of robbers prosper,
And they that provoke God are secure;
That bring their god in their hand.
But ask now the beasts, and they shall teach thee;
And the fowls of the air, and they shall tell thee:
Or speak to the earth, and it shall teach thee;
And the fishes of the sea shall declare unto thee.
Who knoweth not in all these,
That the hand of the LORD hath wrought this?
In whose hand is the soul of every living thing,

*Job again
makes answer
to all three
Friends: Your
common-place
apologies
dishonour God*

And the breath of all mankind.
Doth not the ear try words,
Even as the palate tasteth its meat?
With aged men is wisdom,
And in length of days understanding.
With him is wisdom and might;
He hath counsel and understanding.
Behold, he breaketh down, and it cannot be built
    again;
He shutteth up a man, and there can be no opening.
Behold, he withholdeth the waters, and they dry
    up;
Again, he sendeth them out, and they overturn the
    earth.
With him is strength and effectual working;
The deceived and the deceiver are his.
He leadeth counsellors away spoiled,
And judges maketh he fools.
He looseth the bond of kings,
And bindeth their loins with a girdle.
He leadeth priests away spoiled,
And overthroweth the mighty.
He removeth the speech of the trusty,
And taketh away the understanding of the elders.
He poureth contempt upon princes,
And looseth the belt of the strong.
He discovereth deep things out of darkness,
And bringeth out to light the shadow of death.
He increaseth the nations, and destroyeth them:
He spreadeth the nations abroad, and bringeth them
    in.

He taketh away the heart of the chiefs of the people
   of the earth,
And causeth them to wander in a wilderness where
   there is no way.
They grope in the dark without light,
And he maketh them to stagger like a drunken man.
Lo, mine eye hath seen all this,
Mine ear hath heard and understood it.
What ye know, the same do I know also:
I am not inferior unto you.
Surely I would speak to the Almighty,
And I desire to reason with God.
But ye are forgers of lies,
Ye are all physicians of no value.
Oh that ye would altogether hold your peace!
And it should be your wisdom.
Hear now my reasoning,
And hearken to the pleadings of my lips.
Will ye speak unrighteously for God,
And talk deceitfully for him?
Will ye respect his person?
Will ye contend for God?
Is it good that he should search you out?
Or as one deceiveth a man, will ye deceive him?
He will surely reprove you,
If ye do secretly respect persons.
Shall not his excellency make you afraid,
And his dread fall upon you?
Your memorable sayings are proverbs of ashes,
Your defences are defences of clay.
Hold your peace, let me alone, that I may speak,

And let come on me what will.

to death I am
loyal to him:

At all adventures I will take my flesh in my teeth,
And put my life in mine hand.
Behold, he will slay me; I have no hope:
Nevertheless I will maintain my ways before him.
This also shall be my salvation;
That a godless man shall not come before him.
Hear diligently my speech,
And let my declaration be in your ears.
Behold now, I have ordered my cause;
I know that I shall be justified.
Who is he that will contend with me?
For now if I hold my peace, I shall give up the ghost.
Only do not two things unto me,
Then will I not hide myself from thy face:
Withdraw thine hand far from me;
And let not thy terror make me afraid.
Then call thou, and I will answer;
Or let me speak, and answer thou me.
How many are mine iniquities and sins?
Make me to know my transgression and my sin.
Wherefore hidest thou thy face,
And holdest me for thine enemy?
Wilt thou harass a driven leaf?
And wilt thou pursue the dry stubble?
For thou writest bitter things against me,
And makest me to inherit the iniquities of my youth:
Thou puttest my feet also in the stocks, and markest
    all my paths;
Thou drawest thee a line about the soles of my
    feet:

Though I am like a rotten thing that consumeth,          *though he*
Like a garment that is moth-eaten.          *consumes me*
          *like a thing*
Man that is born of a woman          *that rots:*
Is of few days, and full of trouble.
He cometh forth like a flower, and is cut down:
He fleeth also as a shadow, and continueth not.
And dost thou open thine eyes upon such an one,
And bringest me into judgement with thee?
Who can bring a clean thing out of an unclean? not
     one.
Seeing his days are determined, the number of his
     months is with thee,
And thou hast appointed his bounds that he cannot
     pass;
Look away from him, that he may rest,          *and yet, fain*
          *would I nurse*
Till he shall accomplish, as an hireling, his day.          *some larger*
For there is hope of a tree, if it be cut down, that it          *hope; as some*
          *do…but No,*
     will sprout again,          *it may not be*
And that the tender branch thereof will not cease.
Though the root thereof wax old in the earth,
And the stock thereof die in the ground;
Yet through the scent of water it will bud,
And put forth boughs like a plant.
But man dieth, and wasteth away:
Yea, man giveth up the ghost, and where is he?
As the waters fail from the sea,
And the river decayeth and drieth up;
So man lieth down and riseth not:
Till the heavens be no more, they shall not awake,
Nor be roused out of their sleep.
Oh that thou wouldest hide me in Sheol,

NJ          4

That thou wouldest keep me secret, until thy wrath
    be past,
That thou wouldest appoint me a set time, and re-
    member me!
If a man die, shall he live again?
All the days of my warfare would I wait,
Till my release should come.
Thou shouldest call, and I would answer thee:
Thou wouldest have a desire to the work of thine
    hands.
But now thou numberest my steps:
Dost thou not watch over my sin?
My transgression is sealed up in a bag,
And thou fastenest up mine iniquity.
And surely the mountain falling cometh to nought,
And the rock is removed out of its place;
The waters wear the stones;
The overflowings thereof wash away the dust of the
    earth:
And thou destroyest the hope of man.
Thou prevailest for ever against him, and he passeth;
Thou changest his countenance, and sendest him
    away.
His sons come to honour, and he knoweth it not;
And they are brought low, but he perceiveth it not
    of them.
*...it may not be* But his flesh upon him hath pain,
And his soul within him mourneth.


*Eliphaz answers a second time*     Then answered Eliphaz the Temanite, and said,
Should a wise man make answer with vain knowledge,

And fill his belly with the east wind?
Should he reason with unprofitable talk,
Or with speeches wherewith he can do no good?
Yea, thou doest away with fear,
And restrainest devotion before God.
For thine iniquity teacheth thy mouth,
And thou choosest the tongue of the crafty.
Thine own mouth condemneth thee, and not I;
Yea, thine own lips testify against thee.
Art thou the first man that was born?
Or wast thou brought forth before the hills?
Hast thou heard the secret counsel of God?
And dost thou restrain wisdom to thyself?
What knowest thou, that we know not?
What understandest thou, which is not in us?
With us are both the grayheaded and the very aged
    men,
Much elder than thy father.
Are the consolations of God too small for thee,    Job's words,
And the word that dealeth gently with thee?    he says, are
                                                       blasphemous
Why doth thine heart carry thee away?
And why do thine eyes wink?
That thou turnest thy spirit against God,
And lettest such words go out of thy mouth.
What is man, that he should be clean?
And he which is born of a woman, that he should be
    righteous?
Behold, he putteth no trust in his holy ones;
Yea, the heavens are not clean in his sight.
How much less one that is abominable and corrupt,
A man that drinketh iniquity like water!

sinners do not prosper, as he thinks; their time comes

I will shew thee, hear thou me;
And that which I have seen I will declare:
(Which wise men have told
From their fathers, and have not hid it;
Unto whom alone the land was given,
And no stranger passed among them:)
The wicked man travaileth with pain all his days,
And years that are numbered are laid up for the
    oppressor.
A sound of terrors is in his ears;
In prosperity the spoiler shall come upon him:
He believeth not that he shall return out of darkness,
And he is waited for of the sword:
He wandereth abroad for bread, saying, Where is it?
He knoweth that the day of darkness is ready at his
    hand:
Distress and anguish make him afraid;
They prevail against him, as a king ready to the
    battle:
Because he hath stretched out his hand against God,
And behaveth himself proudly against the Almighty;
He runneth upon him with a stiff neck,
With the thick bosses of his bucklers:
Because he hath covered his face with his fatness,
And made collops of fat on his flanks;
And he hath dwelt in desolate cities,
In houses which no man inhabited,
Which were ready to become heaps.
He shall not be rich, neither shall his substance
    continue,
Neither shall their produce bend to the earth.

He shall not depart out of darkness;
The flame shall dry up his branches,
And by the breath of his mouth shall he go away.
Let him not trust in vanity, deceiving himself:
For vanity shall be his recompence.
It shall be accomplished before his time,
And his branch shall not be green.
He shall shake off his unripe grape as the vine,
And shall cast off his flower as the olive.
For the company of the godless shall be barren,
And fire shall consume the tents of bribery.
They conceive mischief, and bring forth iniquity,
And their belly prepareth deceit.


Then Job answered and said,
I have heard many such things:
Miserable comforters are ye all.
Shall vain words have an end?
Or what provoketh thee that thou answerest?
I also could speak as ye do;
If your soul were in my soul's stead,
I could join words together against you,
And shake mine head at you.
But I would strengthen you with my mouth,
And the solace of my lips should assuage your grief.
Though I speak, my grief is not assuaged:
And though I forbear, what am I eased?
But now he hath made me weary:
Thou hast made desolate all my company.
And thou hast laid fast hold on me, which is a witness
    against me:

*But Job, scorning his Friends,*

*accuseth God of cruel enmity:*

And my leanness riseth up against me, it testifieth to
    my face.
He hath torn me in his wrath, and persecuted me;
He hath gnashed upon me with his teeth:
Mine adversary sharpeneth his eyes upon me.
They have gaped upon me with their mouth;
They have smitten me upon the cheek reproachfully:
They gather themselves together against me.
God delivereth me to the ungodly,
And casteth me into the hands of the wicked.
I was at ease, and he brake me asunder;
Yea, he hath taken me by the neck, and dashed me to
    pieces:
He hath also set me up for his mark.
His archers compass me round about,
He cleaveth my reins asunder, and doth not spare;
He poureth out my gall upon the ground.
He breaketh me with breach upon breach;
He runneth upon me like a giant.
I have sewed sackcloth upon my skin,
And have laid my horn in the dust.
My face is foul with weeping,
And on my eyelids is the shadow of death;
Although there is no violence in mine hands,
And my prayer is pure.
O earth, cover not thou my blood,
And let my cry have no resting place.

*yet pleadeth to God against God,* Even now, behold, my witness is in heaven,
And he that voucheth for me is on high.
My friends scorn me:
But mine eye poureth out tears unto God;

That he would maintain the right of a man with God,
And of a son of man with his neighbour!
For when a few years are come,
I shall go the way whence I shall not return.
My spirit is consumed, my days are extinct,
The grave is ready for me.
Surely there are mockers with me,
And mine eye abideth in their provocation.
Give now a pledge, be surety for me with thyself;
Who is there that will strike hands with me?
For thou hast hid their heart from understanding:
Therefore shalt thou not exalt them.
He that denounceth his friends for a prey,
Even the eyes of his children shall fail.
He hath made me also a byword of the people; *and declares that be God what he will, the righteous man shall hold to his righteousness;*
And I am become an open abhorring.
Mine eye also is dim by reason of sorrow,
And all my members are as a shadow.
Upright men shall be astonied at this,
And the innocent shall stir up himself against the
    godless.
Yet shall the righteous hold on his way,
And he that hath clean hands shall wax stronger and
    stronger.
But return ye, all of you, and come now:
And I shall not find a wise man among you.
My days are past, my purposes are broken off, *though hope fail*
Even the thoughts of my heart.
They change the night into day:
The light, say they, is near unto the darkness.
If I look for Sheol as mine house;

If I have spread my couch in the darkness;
If I have said to corruption, Thou art my father;
To the worm, Thou art my mother, and my sister;
Where then is my hope?
And as for my hope, who shall see it?
It shall go down to the bars of Sheol,
When once there is rest in the dust.

Bildad gravely rejects all such far-fetched entangled mystic talk:

Then answered Bildad the Shuhite, and said,
How long will ye lay snares for words?
Consider, and afterwards we will speak.
Wherefore are we counted as beasts,
And are become unclean in your sight?
Thou that tearest thyself in thine anger,
Shall the earth be forsaken for thee?
Or shall the rock be removed out of its place?

the wicked suffer, and there is an end of argument

Yea, the light of the wicked shall be put out,
And the spark of his fire shall not shine.
The light shall be dark in his tent,
And his lamp above him shall be put out.
The steps of his strength shall be straitened,
And his own counsel shall cast him down.
For he is cast into a net by his own feet,
And he walketh upon the toils.
A gin shall take him by the heel,
And a snare shall lay hold on him.
A noose is hid for him in the ground,
And a trap for him in the way.
Terrors shall make him afraid on every side,
And shall chase him at his heels.
His strength shall be hungerbitten,

And calamity shall be ready for his halting.
It shall devour the members of his body,
Yea, the firstborn of death shall devour his members.
He shall be rooted out of his tent wherein he
    trusteth;
And it shall bring him to the king of terrors.
There shall dwell in his tent that which is none of
    his:
Brimstone shall be scattered upon his habitation.
His roots shall be dried up beneath,
And above shall his branch be cut off.
His remembrance shall perish from the earth,
And he shall have no name in the street.
He shall be driven from light into darkness,
And chased out of the world.
He shall have neither son nor son's son among his
    people,
Nor any remaining where he sojourned.
They that come after shall be astonied at his day,
As they that went before were affrighted.
Surely such are the dwellings of the unrighteous,
And this is the place of him that knoweth not God.


Then Job answered and said,
How long will ye vex my soul,
And break me in pieces with words?
These ten times have ye reproached me:
Ye are not ashamed that ye deal hardly with me.
And be it indeed that I have erred,
Mine error remaineth with myself.
If indeed ye will magnify yourselves against me,

No: answers
Job again;
not the fate
of the wicked,
but the
violence of
God is plain
to see and tell;

And plead against me my reproach:
Know now that God hath subverted me in my cause,
And hath compassed me with his net.
Behold, I cry out, Violence! but I am not heard:
I cry for help, but there is no judgement.
He hath fenced up my way that I cannot pass,
And hath set darkness in my paths.
He hath stripped me of my glory,
And taken the crown from my head.
He hath broken me down on every side, and I am
    gone:
And mine hope hath he plucked up like a tree.
He hath also kindled his wrath against me,
And he counteth me unto him as one of his ad-
    versaries.
His troops come on together, and cast up their way
    against me,
And encamp round about my tent.
He hath put my brethren far from me,
And mine acquaintance are wholly estranged from me.
My kinsfolk have failed,
And my familiar friends have forgotten me.
They that dwell in mine house, and my maids,
    count me for a stranger:
I am an alien in their sight.
I call unto my servant, and he giveth me no answer,
Though I intreat him with my mouth.
My breath is strange to my wife,
And I am loathsome to the children of my body.
Even young children despise me;
If I arise, they speak against me.

All my inward friends abhor me:
And they whom I loved are turned against me.
My bone cleaveth to my skin and to my flesh,
And I am escaped with the skin of my teeth.
Have pity upon me, have pity upon me, O ye my
    friends;
For the hand of God hath touched me.
Why do ye persecute me as God,
And are not satisfied with my flesh?
Oh that my words were now written!
Oh that they were inscribed in a book!
That with an iron pen and lead
They were graven in the rock for ever!
But I know that my redeemer liveth,
And that he shall stand up at the last upon the earth:
And after my skin hath been thus destroyed,
Yet from my flesh shall I see God:
Whom I shall see for myself,
And mine eyes shall behold, and not another.
My reins are consumed within me.
If ye say, How we will persecute him!
And that the root of the matter is found in me;
Be ye afraid of the sword:
For wrath bringeth the punishments of the sword,
That ye may know there is a judgement.

*yet, oh! my Friends, my Friends... nay, God's own self shall vindicate my very self against false friends*

Then answered Zophar the Naamathite, and said,
Therefore do my thoughts give answer to me,
Even by reason of my haste that is in me.
I have heard the reproof which putteth me to shame,
And the spirit of my understanding answereth me.

*To which Zophar breaks forth in wild rhetoric, repeating the old convention: 'Tis the wicked that perish*

Knowest thou not this of old time,
Since man was placed upon earth,
That the triumphing of the wicked is short,
And the joy of the godless but for a moment?
Though his excellency mount up to the heavens,
And his head reach unto the clouds;
Yet he shall perish for ever like his own dung:
They which have seen him shall say, Where is he?
He shall fly away as a dream, and shall not be found:
Yea, he shall be chased away as a vision of the night.
The eye which saw him shall see him no more;
Neither shall his place any more behold him.
His children shall seek the favour of the poor,
And his hands shall give back his wealth.
His bones are full of his youth,
But it shall lie down with him in the dust.
Though wickedness be sweet in his mouth,
Though he hide it under his tongue;
Though he spare it, and will not let it go,
But keep it still within his mouth;
Yet his meat in his bowels is turned,
It is the gall of asps within him.
He hath swallowed down riches, and he shall vomit
    them up again:
God shall cast them out of his belly.
He shall suck the poison of asps:
The viper's tongue shall slay him.
He shall not look upon the rivers,
The flowing streams of honey and butter.
That which he laboured for shall he restore, and shall
    not swallow it down;

According to the substance that he hath gotten, he
    shall not rejoice.
For he hath oppressed and forsaken the poor;
He hath violently taken away an house, and he shall
    not build it up.
Because he knew no quietness in his greed,
He shall not save aught of that wherein he delighteth.
There was nothing left that he devoured not;
Therefore his prosperity shall not endure.
In the fulness of his sufficiency he shall be in straits:
The hand of every one that is in misery shall come
    upon him.
When he is about to fill his belly,
God shall cast the fierceness of his wrath upon
    him,
And shall rain it upon him while he is eating.
He shall flee from the iron weapon,
And the bow of brass shall strike him through.
He draweth it forth, and it cometh out of his
    body:
Yea, the glittering point cometh out of his gall;
Terrors are upon him.
All darkness is laid up for his treasures:
A fire not blown by man shall devour him;
It shall consume that which is left in his tent.
The heavens shall reveal his iniquity,
And the earth shall rise up against him.
The increase of his house shall depart,
His goods shall flow away in the day of his wrath.
This is the portion of a wicked man from God,
And the heritage appointed unto him by God.

Job recalls
attention to the
significance of
plain fact:
let them
diligently
observe; the
wicked are not
the sufferers
as things go;

Then Job answered and said,
Hear diligently my speech;
And let this be your consolations.
Suffer me, and I also will speak;
And after that I have spoken, mock on.
As for me, is my complaint to man?
And why should I not be impatient?
Mark me, and be astonished,
And lay your hand upon your mouth.
Even when I remember I am troubled,
And horror taketh hold on my flesh.
Wherefore do the wicked live,
Become old, yea, wax mighty in power?
Their seed is established with them in their sight,
And their offspring before their eyes.
Their houses are safe from fear,
Neither is the rod of God upon them.
Their bull gendereth, and faileth not;
Their cow calveth, and casteth not her calf.
They send forth their little ones like a flock,
And their children dance.
They sing to the timbrel and harp,
And rejoice at the sound of the pipe.
They spend their days in prosperity,
And in a moment they go down to Sheol.
Yet they said unto God, Depart from us;
For we desire not the knowledge of thy ways.
What is the Almighty, that we should serve him?
And what profit should we have, if we pray unto him?
Lo, their prosperity is not in their hand:
The counsel of the wicked is far from me.

How oft is it that the lamp of the wicked is put out?
That their calamity cometh upon them?
That God distributeth sorrows in his anger?
That they are as stubble before the wind,
And as chaff that the storm carrieth away?
Ye say, God layeth up his iniquity for his children.
Let him recompense it unto himself, that he may
    know it.
Let his own eyes see his destruction,
And let him drink of the wrath of the Almighty.
For what pleasure hath he in his house after him,
When the number of his months is cut off in the
    midst?
Shall any teach God knowledge?
Seeing he judgeth those that are high.
One dieth in his full strength,
Being wholly at ease and quiet:
His milk pails are full of milk,
And the marrow of his bones is moistened.
And another dieth in bitterness of soul,
And never tasteth of good.
They lie down alike in the dust,
And the worm covereth them.
Behold, I know your thoughts,
And the devices which ye wrongfully imagine against
    me.
For ye say, Where is the house of the prince?
And where is the tent wherein the wicked dwelt?
Have ye not asked them that go by the way?
And do ye not know their tokens?
That the evil man is spared in the day of calamity?

God's ways are
mysterious;
your gross
explanations
are faithlessness
towards God

That they are led away in the day of wrath?
Who shall declare his way to his face?
And who shall repay him what he hath done?
Yet shall he be borne to the grave,
And shall keep watch over the tomb.
The clods of the valley shall be sweet unto him,
And all men shall draw after him,
As there were innumerable before him.
How then comfort ye me in vain,
Seeing in your answers there remaineth only false-
hood?

And now
Eliphaz
accuseth Job
directly,

Then answered Eliphaz the Temanite, and said,
Can a man be profitable unto God?
Surely he that is wise is profitable unto himself.
Is it any pleasure to the Almighty, that thou art
righteous?
Or is it gain to him, that thou makest thy ways
perfect?
Is it for thy fear of him that he reproveth thee,
That he entereth with thee into judgement?
Is not thy wickedness great?
Neither is there any end to thine iniquities.
For thou hast taken pledges of thy brother for
nought,
And stripped the naked of their clothing.
Thou hast not given water to the weary to drink,
And thou hast withholden bread from the hungry.
But as for the mighty man, he had the earth;
And the honourable man, he dwelt in it.
Thou hast sent widows away empty,

And the arms of the fatherless have been broken.
Therefore snares are round about thee,
And sudden fear troubleth thee,
Or darkness, that thou canst not see,
And abundance of waters cover thee.
Is not God in the height of heaven?
And behold the height of the stars, how high they are!
And thou sayest, What doth God know?
Can he judge through the thick darkness?
Thick clouds are a covering to him, that he seeth not;
And he walketh in the circuit of heaven.
Wilt thou keep the old way
Which wicked men have trodden?
Who were snatched away before their time,
Whose foundation was poured out as a stream:
Who said unto God, Depart from us;
And, What can the Almighty do for us?
Yet he filled their houses with good things:
But the counsel of the wicked is far from me.
The righteous see it, and are glad;
And the innocent laugh them to scorn:
Saying, Surely they that did rise up against us are cut
     off,
And the remnant of them the fire hath consumed.
Acquaint now thyself with him, and be at peace:     and urgeth
Thereby good shall come unto thee.                        penitence
Receive, I pray thee, the law from his mouth,
And lay up his words in thine heart.
If thou return to the Almighty, thou shalt be built
     up;
If thou put away unrighteousness far from thy tents.

And lay thou thy treasure in the dust,
And the gold of Ophir among the stones of the
    brooks;
And the Almighty shall be thy treasure,
And precious silver unto thee.
For then shalt thou delight thyself in the Almighty,
And shalt lift up thy face unto God.
Thou shalt make thy prayer unto him, and he shall
    hear thee;
And thou shalt pay thy vows.
Thou shalt also decree a thing, and it shall be
    established unto thee;
And light shall shine upon thy ways.
When they cast thee down, thou shalt say, There is
    lifting up;
And the humble person he shall save.
He shall deliver even him that is not innocent:
Yea, he shall be delivered through the cleanness of
    thine hands.

Job turns with deep and serious yearning to God—Oh! that I might find God, he prayeth;

Then Job answered and said,
Even to-day is my complaint rebellious:
My stroke is heavier than my groaning.
Oh that I knew where I might find him,
That I might come even to his seat!
I would order my cause before him,
And fill my mouth with arguments.
I would know the words which he would answer me,
And understand what he would say unto me.
Would he contend with me in the greatness of his
    power?

Nay; but he would give heed unto me.
There the upright might reason with him;
So should I be delivered for ever from my judge.
Behold, I go forward, but he is not there;
And backward, but I cannot perceive him:
On the left hand, when he doth work, but I cannot
    behold him:
He hideth himself on the right hand, that I cannot
    see him.
For he knoweth the way that I take;
When he hath tried me, I shall come forth as gold.
My foot hath held fast to his steps;
His way have I kept, and turned not aside.
I have not gone back from the commandment of his
    lips;
I have treasured up the words of his mouth in my
    bosom.
But he is in one mind, and who can turn him?
And what his soul desireth, even that he doeth.
For he performeth that which is appointed for me:
And many such things are with him.
Therefore am I troubled at his presence;
When I consider, I am afraid of him.
For God hath made my heart faint,
And the Almighty hath troubled me:
For I am not dismayed because of the darkness,
Nor because thick darkness covereth my face.
Why are times not laid up by the Almighty?
And why do not they which know him see his days?
There are that remove the landmarks;
They violently take away flocks, and feed them.

*for the world is wrong and wretched: the poor suffer, and their oppressors prosper and come to a happy end*

They drive away the ass of the fatherless,
They take the widow's ox for a pledge.
They turn the needy out of the way:
The poor of the earth hide themselves together.
Behold, as wild asses in the desert
They go forth to their work, seeking diligently for
    meat;
The wilderness yieldeth them food for their children.
They cut their provender in the field;
And they glean the vintage of the wicked.
They lie all night naked without clothing,
And have no covering in the cold.
They are wet with the showers of the mountains,
And embrace the rock for want of a shelter.
There are that pluck the fatherless from the breast,
And take a pledge of the poor:
So that they go about naked without clothing,
And being an-hungred they carry the sheaves;
They make oil within the walls of these men;
They tread their winepresses, and suffer thirst.
From out of the populous city men groan,
And the soul of the wounded crieth out:
Yet God imputeth it not for folly.
These are of them that rebel against the light;
They know not the ways thereof,
Nor abide in the paths thereof.
The murderer riseth with the light, he killeth the
    poor and needy;
And in the night he is as a thief.
The eye also of the adulterer waiteth for the twi-
    light,

Saying, No eye shall see me:
And he disguiseth his face.
In the dark they dig through houses:
They shut themselves up in the day-time;
They know not the light.
For the morning is to all of them as the shadow of
  death;
For they know the terrors of the shadow of death.
Ye say, He is swift upon the face of the waters;
Their portion is cursed in the earth:
He turneth not by the way of the vineyards.
Drought and heat consume the snow waters:
So doth Sheol those which have sinned.
The womb shall forget him; the worm shall feed
  sweetly on him;
He shall be no more remembered:
And unrighteousness shall be broken as a tree.
He devoureth the barren that beareth not;
And doeth not good to the widow.
He draweth away the mighty also by his power:
He riseth up, and no man is sure of life.
God giveth them to be in security, and they rest
  thereon;
And his eyes are upon their ways.
They are exalted; yet a little while, and they are
  gone;
Yea, they are brought low, they are taken out of the
  way as all other,
And are cut off as the tops of the ears of corn.
And if it be not so now, who will prove me a liar,
And make my speech nothing worth?

Bildad re-
verently closes
the debate

Then answered Bildad the Shuhite, and said,
Dominion and fear are with him;
He maketh peace in his high places.
Is there any number of his armies?
And upon whom doth not his light arise?
How then can man be just with God?
Or how can he be clean that is born of a woman?
Behold, even the moon hath no brightness,
And the stars are not pure in his sight:
How much less man, that is a worm!
And the son of man, which is a worm!

Job ironically
echoes Bildad's
piety

Then Job answered and said,
How hast thou helped him that is without power!
How hast thou saved the arm that hath no strength!
How hast thou counselled him that hath no wisdom,
And plentifully declared sound knowledge!
To whom hast thou uttered words?
And whose spirit came forth from thee?
The shades tremble
Beneath the waters and the inhabitants thereof.
Sheol is naked before him,
And Abaddon* hath no covering.
He stretcheth out the north over empty space,
And hangeth the earth upon nothing.
He bindeth up the waters in his thick clouds;
And the cloud is not rent under them.
He closeth in the face of his throne,
And spreadeth his cloud upon it.

* Or Destruction: like Sheol and Rephaim (the shades),
Rahab and the swift serpent, terms of Hebrew superstition.

He hath described a boundary upon the face of the
    waters,
Unto the confines of light and darkness.
The pillars of heaven tremble
And are astonished at his rebuke.
He stirreth up the sea with his power,
And by his understanding he smiteth through
    Rahab.
By his spirit the heavens are garnished;
His hand hath pierced the swift serpent.
Lo, these are but the outskirts of his ways:
And how small a whisper do we hear of him!
But the thunder of his power who can understand?


And Job again took up his parable, and said,
As God liveth, who hath taken away my right;
And the Almighty, who hath vexed my soul;
(For my life is yet whole in me,
And the spirit of God is in my nostrils;)
Surely my lips shall not speak unrighteousness,
Neither shall my tongue utter deceit.
God forbid that I should justify you:
Till I die I will not put away mine integrity from me.
My righteousness I hold fast, and will not let it go:
My heart shall not reproach me so long as I live.
Let mine enemy be as the wicked,
And let him that riseth up against me be as the un-
    righteous.
For what is the hope of the godless, though he get
    him gain,
When God taketh away his soul?

*And, since Zophar makes no further speech, Job taketh up his parable again, and holdeth fast to his integrity;*

Will God hear his cry,
When trouble cometh upon him?
Will he delight himself in the Almighty,
And call upon God at all times?

turning the
denunciations
of the Friends
upon
themselves

I will teach you concerning the hand of God;
That which is with the Almighty will I not conceal.
Behold, all ye yourselves have seen it;
Why then are ye become altogether vain?
This is the portion of a wicked man with God,
And the heritage of oppressors, which they receive
    from the Almighty.
If his children be multiplied, it is for the sword;
And his offspring shall not be satisfied with bread.
Those that remain of him shall be buried in death,
And his widows shall make no lamentation.
Though he heap up silver as the dust,
And prepare raiment as the clay;
He may prepare it, but the just shall put it on,
And the innocent shall divide the silver.
He buildeth his house as the moth,
And as a booth which the keeper maketh.
He lieth down rich, but he shall not be gathered;
He openeth his eyes, and he is not.
Terrors overtake him like waters;
A tempest stealeth him away in the night.
The east wind carrieth him away, and he departeth;
And it sweepeth him out of his place.
For God shall hurl at him, and not spare:
He would fain flee out of his hand.
Men shall clap their hands at him,
And shall hiss him out of his place.

Surely there is a mine for silver,
And a place for gold which they refine.
Iron is taken out of the earth,
And brass is molten out of the stone.
Man setteth an end to darkness,
And searcheth out to the furthest bound
The stones of thick darkness and of the shadow of
    death.
He breaketh open a shaft away from where men
    sojourn;
They are forgotten of the foot that passeth by;
They hang afar from men, they swing to and fro.
As for the earth, out of it cometh bread:
And underneath it is turned up as it were by fire.
The stones thereof are the place of sapphires,
And it hath dust of gold.
That path no bird of prey knoweth,
Neither hath the falcon's eye seen it:
The proud beasts have not trodden it,
Nor hath the fierce lion passed thereby.
He putteth forth his hand upon the flinty rock;
He overturneth the mountains by the roots.
He cutteth out channels among the rocks;
And his eye seeth every precious thing.
He bindeth the streams that they trickle not;
And the thing that is hid bringeth he forth to
    light.
But where shall wisdom be found?
And where is the place of understanding?
Man knoweth not the price thereof;
Neither is it found in the land of the living.

*Job passeth into meditation on Wisdom: he contemplates man's indomitable labour;*

The deep saith, It is not in me:
And the sea saith, It is not with me.
It cannot be gotten for gold,
Neither shall silver be weighed for the price there-
of.
It cannot be valued with the gold of Ophir,
With the precious onyx, or the sapphire.
Gold and glass cannot equal it:
Neither shall the exchange thereof be jewels of fine
gold.
No mention shall be made of coral or of crystal:
Yea, the price of wisdom is above rubies.
The topaz of Ethiopia shall not equal it,
Neither shall it be valued with pure gold.
Whence then cometh wisdom?
And where is the place of understanding?

and muses on the mystery of his life and death;

Seeing it is hid from the eyes of all living,
And kept close from the fowls of the air.
Destruction and Death say,
We have heard a rumour thereof with our ears.
God understandeth the way thereof,
And he knoweth the place thereof.
For he looketh to the ends of the earth,

but Wisdom is with God the one Creator, and with man in so far as he, reverencing God, may partake of the divine nature

And seeth under the whole heaven;
To make a weight for the wind;
Yea, he meteth out the waters by measure.
When he made a decree for the rain,
And a way for the lightning of the thunder:
Then did he see it, and declare it;
He established it, yea, and searched it out.
And unto man he said,

Behold, the fear of the Lord, that is wisdom;
And to depart from evil is understanding.


And Job again took up his parable, and said,
Oh that I were as in the months of old,
As in the days when God watched over me;
When his lamp shined upon my head,
And by his light I walked through darkness;
As I was in the ripeness of my days,
When the secret of God was upon my tent;
When the Almighty was yet with me,
And my children were about me;
When my steps were washed with butter,
And the rock poured me out rivers of oil!
When I went forth to the gate unto the city,
When I prepared my seat in the street,
The young men saw me and hid themselves,
And the aged rose up and stood;
The princes refrained talking,
And laid their hand on their mouth;
The voice of the nobles was hushed,
And their tongue cleaved to the roof of their mouth.
For when the ear heard me, then it blessed me;
And when the eye saw me, it gave witness unto me:
Because I delivered the poor that cried,
The fatherless also, that had none to help him.
The blessing of him that was ready to perish came
    upon me:
And I caused the widow's heart to sing for joy.
I put on righteousness, and it clothed me:
My justice was as a robe and a diadem.

Such communion, Job continues (after this *Theoria* and *Altitudo*), he once thought was his,

I was eyes to the blind,
And feet was I to the lame.
I was a father to the needy:
And the cause of him that I knew not I searched out.
And I brake the jaws of the unrighteous,
And plucked the prey out of his teeth.
Then I said, I shall die in my nest,
And I shall multiply my days as the sand:
My root is spread out to the waters,
And the dew lieth all night upon my branch:
My glory is fresh in me,
And my bow is renewed in my hand.
Unto me men gave ear, and waited,
And kept silence for my counsel.
After my words they spake not again;
And my speech dropped upon them.
And they waited for me as for the rain;
And they opened their mouth wide as for the latter
    rain.
If I laughed on them, they believed it not;
And the light of my countenance they cast not down.
I chose out their way, and sat as chief,
And dwelt as a king in the army,
As one that comforteth the mourners.

but now God
has turned to
be cruel to him

But now they that are younger than I have me in
    derision,
Whose fathers I disdained to set with the dogs of my
    flock.
Yea, the strength of their hands, whereto should it
    profit me?

Men in whom ripe age is perished.
They are gaunt with want and famine;
They gnaw the dry ground, in the gloom of wasteness
 and desolation.
They pluck salt-wort by the bushes;
And the roots of the broom are their meat.
They are driven forth from the midst of men;
They cry after them as after a thief.
In the clefts of the valleys must they dwell,
In holes of the earth and of the rocks.
Among the bushes they bray;
Under the nettles they are gathered together.
They are children of fools, yea, children of base men;
They were scourged out of the land.
And now I am become their song,
Yea, I am a byword unto them.
They abhor me, they stand aloof from me,
And spare not to spit in my face.
For he hath loosed his cord, and afflicted me,
And they have cast off the bridle before me.
Upon my right hand rise the rabble;
They thrust aside my feet,
And they cast up against me their ways of destruction.
They mar my path,
They set forward my calamity,
Even men that have no helper.
As through a wide breach they come:
In the midst of the ruin they roll themselves upon me.
Terrors are turned upon me,
They chase mine honour as the wind;
And my welfare is passed away as a cloud.

And now my soul is poured out within me;
Days of affliction have taken hold upon me.
In the night season my bones are pierced in me,
And the pains that gnaw me take no rest.
By the great force of my disease is my garment dis-
  figured:
It bindeth me about as the collar of my coat.
He hath cast me into the mire,
And I am become like dust and ashes.
I cry unto thee, and thou dost not answer me:
I stand up, and thou lookest at me.
Thou art turned to be cruel to me:
With the might of thy hand thou persecutest me.
Thou liftest me up to the wind, thou causest me to
  ride upon it;
And thou dissolvest me in the storm.
For I know that thou wilt bring me to death,
And to the house appointed for all living.
Howbeit doth not one stretch out the hand in his
  fall?
Or in his calamity therefore cry for help?
Did not I weep for him that was in trouble?
Was not my soul grieved for the needy?
When I looked for good, then evil came;
And when I waited for light, there came darkness.
My bowels boil, and rest not;
Days of affliction are come upon me.
I go mourning without the sun:
I stand up in the assembly, and cry for help.
I am a brother to jackals,
And a companion to ostriches.

My skin is black, and falleth from me,
And my bones are burned with heat.
Therefore is my harp turned to mourning,
And my pipe into the voice of them that weep.

I made a covenant with mine eyes;
How then should I look upon a maid?
For what is the portion of God from above,
And the heritage of the Almighty from on high?
Is it not calamity to the unrighteous,
And disaster to the workers of iniquity?
Doth not he see my ways,
And number all my steps?
If I have walked with vanity,
And my foot hath hasted to deceit;
(Let me be weighed in an even balance,
That God may know mine integrity;)
If my step hath turned out of the way,
And mine heart walked after mine eyes,
And if any spot hath cleaved to mine hands:
Then let me sow, and let another eat;
Yea, let the produce of my field be rooted out.
If mine heart have been enticed unto a woman,
And I have laid wait at my neighbour's door:
Then let my wife grind unto another,
And let others bow down upon her.
For that were an heinous crime;
Yea, it were an iniquity to be punished by the
    judges:
For it is a fire that consumeth unto Destruction,
And would root out all mine increase.

Yet Job
repudiates the
vile accusations
of his Friends,

If I did despise the cause of my manservant or of my
    maidservant,
When they contended with me:
What then shall I do when God riseth up?
And when he visiteth, what shall I answer him?
Did not he that made me in the womb make him?
And did not one fashion us in the womb?
If I have withheld the poor from their desire,
Or have caused the eyes of the widow to fail;
Or have eaten my morsel alone,
And the fatherless hath not eaten thereof;
(Nay, from my youth he grew up with me as with a
    father,
And I have been her guide from my mother's womb;)
If I have seen any perish for want of clothing,
Or that the needy had no covering;
If his loins have not blessed me,
And if he were not warmed with the fleece of my
    sheep;
If I have lifted up my hand against the fatherless,
Because I saw my help in the gate:
Then let my shoulder fall from the shoulder blade,
And mine arm be broken from the bone.
For calamity from God was a terror to me,
And by reason of his excellency I could do nothing.
If I have made gold my hope,
And have said to the fine gold, Thou art my con-
    fidence;
If I rejoiced because my wealth was great,
And because mine hand had gotten much;
If I beheld the sun when it shined,

Or the moon walking in brightness;
And my heart hath been secretly enticed,
And my mouth hath kissed my hand:
This also were an iniquity to be punished by the
      judges:
For I should have lied to God that is above.
If I rejoiced at the destruction of him that hated me,
Or lifted up myself when evil found him;
(Yea, I suffered not my mouth to sin
By asking his life with a curse;)
If the men of my tent said not,
Who can find one that hath not been satisfied with
      his flesh?
The stranger did not lodge in the street;
But I opened my doors to the traveller;
If after the manner of men I covered my trans-
      gressions,
By hiding mine iniquity in my bosom;
Because I feared the great multitude,
And the contempt of families terrified me,
So that I kept silence, and went not out of the door—
Oh that I had one to hear me!
(Lo, here is my signature, let the Almighty answer
      me;)
And that I had the indictment which mine adversary
      hath written!
Surely I would carry it upon my shoulder;
I would bind it unto me as a crown.
I would declare unto him the number of my steps;
As a prince would I go near unto him.
If my land cry out against me,

and calls the Almighty to witness and to answer his appeal—and at once (in chapter xxxviii) Jahveh does answer out of the whirlwind

And the furrows thereof weep together;
If I have eaten the fruits thereof without money,
Or have caused the owners thereof to lose their life:
Let thistles grow instead of wheat,
And cockle instead of barley.

The words of Job are ended.

For in
chapters xxxii–
xxxvii Elihu's
intervention
interrupts the
story and its
meaning: his
words hang in
empty space,
ignored by
God and man:
he has merits;
he intervenes
with youthful
modesty and
confidence,
and brings a
certain fresh-air
amenity across
the terrible
intensity of the
drama,

So these three men ceased to answer Job, because
he was righteous in his own eyes. Then was kindled
the wrath of Elihu the son of Barachel the Buzite, of
the family of Ram: against Job was his wrath kindled,
because he justified himself rather than God. Also
against his three friends was his wrath kindled, because
they had found no answer, and yet had condemned
Job. Now Elihu had waited to speak unto Job, because they were elder than he. And when Elihu saw
that there was no answer in the mouth of these three
men, his wrath was kindled.

And Elihu the son of Barachel the Buzite answered
and said,
I am young, and ye are very old;
Wherefore I held back, and durst not shew you mine
    opinion.
I said, Days should speak,
And multitude of years should teach wisdom.
But there is a spirit in man,
And the breath of the Almighty giveth them under-
    standing.
It is not the great that are wise,
Nor the aged that understand judgement.

For God speaketh once yea twice
& Man perceiveth it not

In a Dream in a Vision of the Night
in deep Slumberings upon the bed
Then he openeth the ears of Men & sealeth their instruction

That he may withdraw Man from his purpose
& hide Pride from Man

If there be with him an Interpreter One among a Thousand
then he is gracious unto him
& saith Deliver him from going down to the Pit
I have found a Ransom

For his eyes are upon
the ways of Man & he observeth
all his goings

I am Young & ye are very Old wherefore I was afraid

Lo all these things worketh God oftentimes with Man to bring
back his Soul from the pit to be enlightened
with the light of the living

Look upon the heavens & behold the clouds
which are higher
than thou

If thou sinnest what
doest thou against him. or if thou be
righteous what givest thou unto him

WBlake invenit & sculpt

London. Published as the Act directs March 8:1825 by Will Blake N 3 Fountain Court Strand

Proof

Therefore I said, Hearken to me;
I also will shew mine opinion.
Behold, I waited for your words,
I listened for your reasons,
Whilst ye searched out what to say.
Yea, I attended unto you,
And, behold, there was none that convinced Job,
Or that answered his words, among you.
Beware lest ye say, We have found wisdom;
God may vanquish him, not man:
For he hath not directed his words against me;
Neither will I answer him with your speeches.
They are amazed, they answer no more:
They have not a word to say.
And shall I wait, because they speak not,
Because they stand still, and answer no more?
I also will answer my part,
I also will shew mine opinion.
For I am full of words;
The spirit within me constraineth me.
Behold, my belly is as wine which hath no vent;
Like new bottles it is ready to burst.
I will speak, that I may be refreshed;
I will open my lips and answer.
Let me not, I pray you, respect any man's person;
Neither will I give flattering titles unto any man.
For I know not to give flattering titles;
Else would my Maker soon take me away.
Howbeit, Job, I pray thee, hear my speech,
And hearken to all my words.
Behold now, I have opened my mouth,

My tongue hath spoken in my mouth.
My words shall utter the uprightness of my heart:
And that which my lips know they shall speak
    sincerely.
The spirit of God hath made me,
And the breath of the Almighty giveth me life.
If thou canst, answer thou me;
Set thy words in order before me, stand forth.
Behold, I am toward God even as thou art:
I also am formed out of the clay.
Behold, my terror shall not make thee afraid,
Neither shall my pressure be heavy upon thee.

*but has little to say beyond commonplaces of the newer fashion;*

Surely thou hast spoken in mine hearing,
And I have heard the voice of thy words, saying,
I am clean, without transgression;
I am innocent, neither is there iniquity in me:
Behold, he findeth occasions against me,
He counteth me for his enemy;
He putteth my feet in the stocks,
He marketh all my paths.
Behold, I will answer thee, in this thou art not just;
For God is greater than man.
Why dost thou strive against him?
For he giveth not account of any of his matters.

*especially that suffering is remedial;*

For God speaketh once,
Yea twice, though man regardeth it not.
In a dream, in a vision of the night,
When deep sleep falleth upon men,
In slumberings upon the bed;
Then he openeth the ears of men,
And sealeth their instruction,

That he may withdraw man from his purpose,
And hide pride from man;
He keepeth back his soul from the pit,
And his life from perishing by the sword.
He is chastened also with pain upon his bed,
And with continual strife in his bones:
So that his life abhorreth bread,
And his soul dainty meat.
His flesh is consumed away, that it cannot be seen;
And his bones that were not seen stick out.
Yea, his soul draweth near unto the pit,
And his life to the destroyers.
If there be with him an angel,
An interpreter, one among a thousand,
To shew unto man what is right for him;
Then he is gracious unto him, and saith,
Deliver him from going down to the pit,
I have found a ransom.
His flesh shall be fresher than a child's;
He returneth to the days of his youth:
He prayeth unto God, and he is favourable unto him;
So that he seeth his face with joy:
And he restoreth unto man his righteousness.
He singeth before men, and saith,
I have sinned, and perverted that which was right,
And it profited me not:
He hath redeemed my soul from going into the pit,
And my life shall behold the light.
Lo, all these things doth God work,
Twice, yea thrice, with a man,
To bring back his soul from the pit,

That he may be enlightened with the light of the
    living.
Mark well, O Job, hearken unto me:
Hold thy peace, and I will speak.
If thou hast any thing to say, answer me:
Speak, for I desire to justify thee.
If not, hearken thou unto me:
Hold thy peace, and I will teach thee wisdom.

Moreover Elihu answered and said,
Hear my words, ye wise men;
And give ear unto me, ye that have knowledge.
For the ear trieth words,
As the palate tasteth meat.
Let us choose for us that which is right:
Let us know among ourselves what is good.
For Job hath said, I am righteous,
And God hath taken away my right:
Notwithstanding my right I am accounted a liar;
My wound is incurable, though I am without trans-
    gression.
What man is like Job,
Who drinketh up scorning like water?
Which goeth in company with the workers of
    iniquity,
And walketh with wicked men.
For he hath said, It profiteth a man nothing
That he should delight himself with God.

*and God is*
*always good;*  Therefore hearken unto me, ye men of under-
    standing:
Far be it from God, that he should do wickedness;

And from the Almighty, that he should commit
   iniquity.
For the work of a man shall he render unto him,
And cause every man to find according to his ways.
Yea, of a surety, God will not do wickedly,
Neither will the Almighty pervert judgement.
Who gave him a charge over the earth?
Or who hath disposed the whole world?
If he set his heart upon himself,
If he gather unto himself his spirit and his breath;
All flesh shall perish together,
And man shall turn again unto dust.
If now thou hast understanding, hear this:
Hearken to the voice of my words.
Shall even one that hateth right govern?
And wilt thou condemn him that is just and mighty?
Who saith to a king, Thou art vile?
Or to nobles, Ye are wicked;
That respecteth not the persons of princes,
Nor regardeth the rich more than the poor?
For they all are the work of his hands.
In a moment they die, even at midnight;
The people are shaken and pass away,
And the mighty are taken away without hand.
For his eyes are upon the ways of a man,
And he seeth all his goings.
There is no darkness, nor shadow of death,
Where the workers of iniquity may hide them-
   selves.
For he needeth not further to consider a man,
That he should go before God in judgement.

He breaketh in pieces mighty men without inquisi-
tion,
And setteth others in their stead.
Therefore he taketh knowledge of their works;
And he overturneth them in the night, so that they
are destroyed.
He striketh them as wicked men
In the open sight of others;
Because they turned aside from following him,
And would not have regard to any of his ways:
So that they caused the cry of the poor to come unto
him,
And he heard the cry of the afflicted.
When he giveth quietness, who then can condemn?
And when he hideth his face, who then can behold
him?
Whether it be done unto a nation, or unto a man,
alike:
That the godless man reign not,
That there be none to ensnare the people.
For hath any said unto God,
I have borne chastisement, I will not offend any
more:
That which I see not teach thou me:
If I have done iniquity, I will do it no more?
Shall his recompence be as thou wilt, that thou re-
fusest it?
For thou must choose, and not I:
Therefore speak what thou knowest.
Men of understanding will say unto me,
Yea, every wise man that heareth me:

Job speaketh without knowledge,
And his words are without wisdom.
Would that Job were tried unto the end,
Because of his answering like wicked men.
For he addeth rebellion unto his sin,
He clappeth his hands among us,
And multiplieth his words against God.


Moreover Elihu answered and said,
Thinkest thou this to be thy right,
Or sayest thou, My righteousness is more than God's,
That thou sayest, What advantage will it be unto
    thee?
And, What profit shall I have, more than if I had
    sinned?
I will answer thee,
And thy companions with thee.
Look unto the heavens, and see;                    and merit lives
And behold the skies, which are higher than thou.  from man to
                                                   man, but not
If thou hast sinned, what doest thou against him?  from man to
                                                   God:
And if thy transgressions be multiplied, what doest
    thou unto him?
If thou be righteous, what givest thou him?
Or what receiveth he of thine hand?
Thy wickedness may hurt a man as thou art;
And thy righteousness may profit a son of man.
By reason of the multitude of oppressions they cry
    out;
They cry for help by reason of the arm of the mighty.
But none saith, Where is God my Maker,
Who giveth songs in the night;

Who teacheth us more than the beasts of the earth,
And maketh us wiser than the fowls of heaven?
There they cry, but none giveth answer,
Because of the pride of evil men.
Surely God will not hear vanity,
Neither will the Almighty regard it.
How much less when thou sayest thou beholdest him
   not,
The cause is before him, and thou waitest for him!
But now, because he hath not visited in his anger,
Neither doth he greatly regard arrogance;
Therefore doth Job open his mouth in vanity;
He multiplieth words without knowledge.

Elihu also proceeded, and said,
Suffer me a little, and I will shew thee;
For I have yet somewhat to say on God's behalf.
I will fetch my knowledge from afar,
And will ascribe righteousness to my Maker.
For truly my words are not false:
One that is perfect in knowledge is with thee.
Behold, God is mighty, and despiseth not any:
He is mighty in strength of understanding.
He preserveth not the life of the wicked:
But giveth to the afflicted their right.
He withdraweth not his eyes from the righteous:
But with kings upon the throne
He setteth them for ever, and they are exalted.
And if they be bound in fetters,
And be taken in the cords of affliction;
Then he sheweth them their work,

And their transgressions, that they have behaved
   themselves proudly.
He openeth also their ear to instruction,
And commandeth that they return from iniquity.
If they hearken and serve him,
They shall spend their days in prosperity,
And their years in pleasures.
But if they hearken not, they shall perish by the
   sword,
And they shall die without knowledge.
But they that are godless in heart lay up anger:
They cry not for help when he bindeth them.
They die in youth,
And their life perisheth among the unclean.
He delivereth the afflicted by his affliction,
And openeth their ear in oppression.
Yea, he would have allured thee out of distress
Into a broad place, where there is no straitness;
And that which is set on thy table should be full of
   fatness.
But thou art full of the judgement of the wicked:
Judgement and justice take hold on thee.
For beware lest wrath allure thee into mockery;
Neither let the greatness of the ransom turn thee
   aside.
Will thy riches suffice, that thou be not in distress,
Or all the forces of thy strength?
Desire not the night,
When peoples are cut off in their place.
Take heed, regard not iniquity:
For this hast thou chosen rather than affliction.

God is a lofty
teacher, says
Elihu,
Behold, God doeth loftily in his power:
Who is a teacher like unto him?
Who hath enjoined him his way?
Or who can say, Thou hast wrought unrighteousness?
Remember that thou magnify his work,
Whereof men have sung.
All men have looked thereon;
Man beholdeth it afar off.
Behold, God is great, and we know him not;
The number of his years is unsearchable.
For he draweth up the drops of water,
Which distil in rain from his vapour:
Which the skies pour down
And drop upon man abundantly.

and behold!
even now
he cometh in
the storm:
Yea, can any understand the spreadings of the clouds,
The thunderings of his pavilion?
Behold, he spreadeth his light around him;
And he covereth the bottom of the sea.
For by these he judgeth the peoples;
He giveth meat in abundance.
He covereth his hands with the lightning;
And giveth it a charge that it strike the mark.
The noise thereof telleth concerning him,
The cattle also concerning the storm that cometh up.
At this also my heart trembleth,
And is moved out of its place.
Hearken ye unto the noise of his voice,
And the sound that goeth out of his mouth.
He sendeth it forth under the whole heaven,
And his lightning unto the ends of the earth.
After it a voice roareth;

He thundereth with the voice of his majesty:
And he stayeth them not when his voice is heard.
God thundereth marvellously with his voice;
Great things doeth he, which we cannot comprehend.
For he saith to the snow, Fall thou on the earth;
Likewise to the shower of rain,
And to the showers of his mighty rain.
He sealeth up the hand of every man;
That all men whom he hath made may know it.
Then the beasts go into coverts,
And remain in their dens.
Out of the chamber of the south cometh the storm:
And cold out of the north.
By the breath of God ice is given:
And the breadth of the waters is straitened.
Yea, he ladeth the thick cloud with moisture;
He spreadeth abroad the cloud of his lightning:
And it is turned round about by his guidance,
That they may do whatsoever he commandeth them
Upon the face of the habitable world:
Whether it be for correction, or for his land,
Or for mercy, that he cause it to come.
Hearken unto this, O Job:
Stand still, and consider the wondrous works of God.
Dost thou know how God layeth his charge upon
    them,
And causeth the lightning of his cloud to shine?
Dost thou know the balancings of the clouds,
The wondrous works of him which is perfect in
    knowledge?
How thy garments are warm,

When the earth is still by reason of the south wind?
Canst thou with him spread out the sky,
Which is strong as a molten mirror?
Teach us what we shall say unto him;
For we cannot order our speech by reason of darkness.
Shall it be told him that I would speak?
Or should a man wish that he were swallowed up?

*thus linking the episode with the main text* And now men see not the light which is bright in the skies:
But the wind passeth, and cleanseth them.
Out of the north cometh golden splendour:
God hath upon him terrible majesty.
Touching the Almighty, we cannot find him out; he is excellent in power:
And to judgement and plenteous justice he doeth no violence.
Men do therefore fear him:
He regardeth not any that are wise of heart.

*Jahveh displays the wonder of Creation,* Then the LORD answered Job out of the whirlwind, and said,
Who is this that darkeneth counsel
By words without knowledge?
Gird up now thy loins like a man;
For I will demand of thee, and declare thou unto me.
Where wast thou when I laid the foundations of the earth?
Declare, if thou hast understanding.
Who determined the measures thereof, if thou knowest?
Or who stretched the line upon it?

Canst thou bind the sweet influences of Pleiades or loose the bands of Orion

Let there Be

Light

Let there be A

Firmament

Let the Waters be gathered together into one place

& let the Dry Land appear

And God made Two Great Lights

Sun

Moon

Let the Waters bring forth abundantly

Let the Earth bring forth

Cattle & Creeping thing & Beast

When the morning Stars sang together, & all the
Sons of God shouted for joy

W Blake Inv & et Sc

London, Published as the Act directs March 8. 1825 by Will Blake N.3 Fountain Court Strand

Whereupon were the foundations thereof fastened?
Or who laid the corner stone thereof;
When the morning stars sang together,
And all the sons of God shouted for joy?
Or who shut up the sea with doors,
When it brake forth, as if it had issued out of the
    womb;
When I made the cloud the garment thereof,
And thick darkness a swaddlingband for it,
And prescribed for it my decree,
And set bars and doors,
And said, Hitherto shalt thou come, but no further;
And here shall thy proud waves be stayed?
Hast thou commanded the morning since thy days
    began,
And caused the dayspring to know its place;
That it might take hold of the ends of the earth,
And the wicked be shaken out of it?
It is changed as clay under the seal;
And all things stand forth as a garment:
And from the wicked their light is withholden,
And the high arm is broken.
Hast thou entered into the springs of the sea?
Or hast thou walked in the recesses of the deep?
Have the gates of death been revealed unto thee?
Or hast thou seen the gates of the shadow of death?
Hast thou comprehended the breadth of the earth?
Declare, if thou knowest it all.
Where is the way to the dwelling of light,
And as for darkness, where is the place thereof;
That thou shouldest take it to the bound thereof,

And that thou shouldest discern the paths to the
  house thereof?
Doubtless, thou knowest, for thou wast then born,
And the number of thy days is great!
Hast thou entered the treasuries of the snow,
Or hast thou seen the treasuries of the hail,
Which I have reserved against the time of trouble,
Against the day of battle and war?
By what way is the light parted,
Or the east wind scattered upon the earth?
Who hath cleft a channel for the waterflood,
Or a way for the lightning of the thunder;
To cause it to rain on a land where no man is;
On the wilderness, wherein there is no man;
To satisfy the waste and desolate ground;
And to cause the tender grass to spring forth?
Hath the rain a father?
Or who hath begotten the drops of dew?
Out of whose womb came the ice?
And the hoary frost of heaven, who hath gendered it?
The waters are hidden as with stone,
And the face of the deep is frozen.
Canst thou bind the cluster of the Pleiades,
Or loose the bands of Orion?
Canst thou lead forth the Mazzaroth* in their
  season?
Or canst thou guide the Bear with her train?
Knowest thou the ordinances of the heavens?
Canst thou establish the dominion thereof in the
  earth?

  * Perhaps = signs of Zodiac, cf. 2 Kings xxiii. 5.

Canst thou lift up thy voice to the clouds,
That abundance of waters may cover thee?
Canst thou send forth lightnings, that they may go,
And say unto thee, Here we are?
Who hath put wisdom in the dark clouds?
Or who hath given understanding to the meteor?
Who can number the clouds by wisdom?
Or who can pour out the bottles of heaven,
When the dust runneth into a mass,
And the clods cleave fast together?

    Wilt thou hunt the prey for the lioness?
Or satisfy the appetite of the young lions,
When they couch in their dens,
And abide in the covert to lie in wait?

    Who provideth for the raven his food,
When his young ones cry unto God,
And wander for lack of meat?
Knowest thou the time when the wild goats of the
    rock bring forth?
Or canst thou mark when the hinds do calve?
Canst thou number the months that they fulfil?
Or knowest thou the time when they bring forth?
They bow themselves, they bring forth their young,
They cast out their sorrows.
Their young ones are in good liking, they grow up in
    the open field;
They go forth, and return not again.

    Who hath sent out the wild ass free?
Or who hath loosed the bands of the wild ass?
Whose house I have made the wilderness,
And the salt land his dwelling place.

He scorneth the tumult of the city,
Neither heareth he the shoutings of the driver.
The range of the mountains is his pasture,
And he searcheth after every green thing.
　　Will the wild-ox be content to serve thee?
Or will he abide by thy crib?
Canst thou bind the wild-ox with his band in the
　　furrow?
Or will he harrow the valleys after thee?
Wilt thou trust him, because his strength is great?
Or wilt thou leave to him thy labour?
Wilt thou confide in him, that he will bring home thy
　　seed,
And gather the corn of thy threshingfloor?
　　The wing of the ostrich rejoiceth;
But are her pinions and feathers kindly?
For she leaveth her eggs on the earth,
And warmeth them in the dust,
And forgetteth that the foot may crush them,
Or that the wild beast may trample them.
She is hardened against her young ones, as if they
　　were not hers:
Though her labour be in vain, she is without fear;
Because God hath deprived her of wisdom,
Neither hath he imparted to her understanding.
What time she lifteth up herself on high,
She scorneth the horse and his rider.
　　Hast thou given the horse his might?
Hast thou clothed his neck with the quivering mane?
Hast thou made him to leap as a locust?
The glory of his snorting is terrible.

He paweth in the valley, and rejoiceth in his strength:
He goeth out to meet the armed men.
He mocketh at fear, and is not dismayed;
Neither turneth he back from the sword.
The quiver rattleth against him,
The flashing spear and the javelin.
He swalloweth the ground with fierceness and rage;
Neither standeth he still at the voice of the trumpet.
As oft as the trumpet soundeth he saith, Aha!
And he smelleth the battle afar off,
The thunder of the captains, and the shouting.
    Doth the hawk soar by thy wisdom,
And stretch her wings toward the south?
Doth the eagle mount up at thy command,
And make her nest on high?
She dwelleth on the rock, and hath her lodging there,
Upon the crag of the rock, and the strong hold.
From thence she spieth out the prey;
Her eyes behold it afar off.
Her young ones also suck up blood:
And where the slain are, there is she.


Moreover the LORD answered Job, and said,     *and asks Job whether he will still cavil*
Shall he that cavilleth contend with the Almighty?
He that argueth with God, let him answer it.


Then Job answered the LORD, and said,
Behold, I am of small account; what shall I answer     *Job can make no reply*
    thee?
I lay mine hand upon my mouth.

Once have I spoken, and I will not answer;
Yea twice, but I will proceed no further.

Jahveh
resumes his
overwhelming
revelation:
Then the LORD answered Job out of the whirlwind,
and said,
Gird up thy loins now like a man:
I will demand of thee, and declare thou unto me.
Wilt thou even disannul my judgement?
Wilt thou condemn me, that thou mayest be justified?
Can Job rule
the proud and
froward world?
Or hast thou an arm like God?
And canst thou thunder with a voice like him?
Deck thyself now with excellency and dignity;
And array thyself with honour and majesty.
Pour forth the overflowings of thine anger:
And look upon every one that is proud, and abase
    him.
Look on every one that is proud, and bring him low;
And tread down the wicked where they stand.
Hide them in the dust together;
Bind their faces in the hidden place.
which is
typified by
two monstrous
Powers of
Nature: Brute
Force and
Arrogance,
shadowed
forth in the
Beasts of the
River,
embroidered in
pictures of old
mythology,
illustrated in
the history of
empires
Then will I also confess of thee
That thine own right hand can save thee.
Behold now behemoth, which I made with thee;
He eateth grass as an ox.
Lo now, his strength is in his loins,
And his force is in the muscles of his belly.
He moveth his tail like a cedar:
The sinews of his thighs are knit together.
His bones are as tubes of brass;
His limbs are like bars of iron.
He is the chief of the ways of God:

He only that made him can make his sword to
  approach unto him.
Surely the mountains bring him forth food;
Where all the beasts of the field do play.
He lieth under the lotus trees,
In the covert of the reed, and the fen.
The lotus trees cover him with their shadow;
The willows of the brook compass him about.
Behold, if a river overflow, he trembleth not:
He is confident, though Jordan swell even to his
  mouth.
Shall any take him when he is on the watch,
Or pierce through his nose with a snare?
     Canst thou draw out leviathan with a fish hook?
Or press down his tongue with a cord?
Canst thou put a rope into his nose?
Or pierce his jaw through with a hook?
Will he make many supplications unto thee?
Or will he speak soft words unto thee?
Will he make a covenant with thee,
That thou shouldest take him for a servant for ever?
Wilt thou play with him as with a bird?
Or wilt thou bind him for thy maidens?
Shall the bands of fishermen make traffic of him?
Shall they part him among the merchants?
Canst thou fill his skin with barbed irons,
Or his head with fish spears?
Lay thine hand upon him;
Remember the battle, and do so no more.
Behold, the hope of him is in vain:
Shall not one be cast down even at the sight of him?

None is so fierce that he dare stir him up:
Who then is he that can stand before me?
Who hath first given unto me, that I should repay
    him?
Whatsoever is under the whole heaven is mine.
I will not keep silence concerning his limbs,
Nor his mighty strength, nor his comely proportion.
Who can strip off his outer garment?
Who shall come within his double bridle?
Who can open the doors of his face?
Round about his teeth is terror.
His strong scales are his pride,
Shut up together as with a close seal.
One is so near to another,
That no air can come between them.
They are joined one to another;
They stick together, that they cannot be sundered.
His neesings flash forth light,
And his eyes are like the eyelids of the morning.
Out of his mouth go burning torches,
And sparks of fire leap forth.
Out of his nostrils a smoke goeth,
As of a seething pot and burning rushes.
His breath kindleth coals,
And a flame goeth forth from his mouth.
In his neck abideth strength,
And terror danceth before him.
The flakes of his flesh are joined together:
They are firm upon him; they cannot be moved.
His heart is as firm as a stone;
Yea, firm as the nether millstone.

When he raiseth himself up, the mighty are afraid:
By reason of consternation they are beside them-
    selves.
If one lay at him with the sword, it cannot avail;
Nor the spear, the dart, nor the pointed shaft.
He counteth iron as straw,
And brass as rotten wood.
The arrow cannot make him flee:
Slingstones are turned with him into stubble.
Clubs are counted as stubble:
He laugheth at the rushing of the javelin.
His underparts are like sharp potsherds:
He spreadeth as it were a threshing wain upon the
    mire.
He maketh the deep to boil like a pot:
He maketh the sea like ointment.
He maketh a path to shine after him;
One would think the deep to be hoary.
Upon earth there is not his like,
That is made without fear.
He beholdeth every thing that is high:
He is king over all the sons of pride.


Then Job answered the LORD, and said,
I know that thou canst do all things,
And that no purpose of thine can be restrained.
Who is this that hideth counsel without knowledge?
Therefore have I uttered that which I understood
    not,
Things too wonderful for me, which I knew not.
Hear, I beseech thee, and I will speak;

Job now knows
God as never
before, and
bows beneath
his majesty,
undone but
new born,
converted out
of death to life

I will demand of thee, and declare thou unto me.
I had heard of thee by the hearing of the ear;
But now mine eye seeth thee,
Wherefore I loathe my words, and repent
In dust and ashes.

a happy
Epilogue

And it was so, that after the LORD had spoken these words unto Job, the LORD said to Eliphaz the Temanite, My wrath is kindled against thee, and against thy two friends: for ye have not spoken of me the thing that is right, as my servant Job hath. Now therefore, take unto you seven bullocks and seven rams, and go to my servant Job, and offer up for yourselves a burnt offering; and my servant Job shall pray for you; for him will I accept, that I deal not with you after your folly; for ye have not spoken of me the thing that is right, as my servant Job hath. So Eliphaz the Temanite and Bildad the Shuhite and Zophar the Naamathite went, and did according as the LORD commanded them: and the LORD accepted Job. And the LORD turned the captivity of Job, when he prayed for his friends: and the LORD gave Job twice as much as he had before. Then came there unto him all his brethren, and all his sisters, and all they that had been of his acquaintance before, and did eat bread with him in his house: and they bemoaned him, and comforted him concerning all the evil that the LORD had brought upon him: every man also gave him a piece of money, and every one a ring of gold. So the LORD blessed the latter end of Job more than his beginning: and he had fourteen thou-

Also the Lord accepted Job

And my Servant Job shall pray for you

And the Lord turned the captivity of Job when he prayed for his Friends

W Blake inv &
sculp

London Published as the Act directs March 8 1825 by Will Blake N 3 Fountain Court Strand

Proof

sand sheep, and six thousand camels, and a thousand yoke of oxen, and a thousand she-asses. He had also seven sons and three daughters. And he called the name of the first, Jemimah; and the name of the second, Keziah; and the name of the third, Keren-happuch. And in all the land were no women found so fair as the daughters of Job: and their father gave them inheritance among their brethren. And after this Job lived an hundred and forty years, and saw his sons, and his sons' sons, even four generations. So Job died, being old and full of days.

CPSIA information can be obtained at www.ICGtesting.com
Printed in the USA
LVOW01s0505240913

353756LV00007B/89/P